THE
AGE OF
HIROHITO

THE AGE
of
HIROHITO

In Search of Modern Japan

DAIKICHI IROKAWA

Translated by Mikiso Hane and John K. Urda
Foreword by Carol Gluck

THE FREE PRESS

NEW YORK   LONDON   TORONTO   SYDNEY   TOKYO   SINGAPORE

The Free Press
A Division of Simon & Schuster Inc.
1230 Avenue of the Americas, New York, N.Y. 10020

Printed in the United States of America

printing number
1 2 3 4 5 6 7 8 9 10

Library of Congress Cataloging-in-Publication Data
Irokawa, Daikichi
  [Shōwa shi to Tennō.   English]
  The age of Hirohito: in search of modern Japan/ Daikichi Irokawa;
  translated by Mikiso Hane and John K. Urda; foreword by Carol Gluck.
    p.   cm.
  Includes index.
  ISBN 0-02-915665-3
    1. Japan—History—Shōwa period, 1926–1989.   2. Hirohito, Emperor
  of Japan, 1901–1989.   I. Hane, Mikiso.   II. Title.
  DS888.2.I758   1995
  952.03'3—dc20   94-47594
                                                                        CIP

Japanese names in the text are given in Japanese order, that is, surname first and given name second.

In the transcription of Japanese words, macrons are used to denote long vowels (except in the case of well-known place-names). Chinese has been romanized according to the pinyin system.

CONTENTS

Foreword by Carol Gluck   vii

Preface to the English Edition   xiii

Introduction: The Limits of Contemporary History   3

Chapter 1   War and Peace   5

Chapter 2   The Lifestyle Revolution   40

Chapter 3   The Emperor and the People   71

Chapter 4   The Symbolic Emperor   108

Chapter 5   Facing the Twenty-First Century   138

Appendix: Excerpt from the Constitution of Japan   147

Index   153

FOREWORD

Since 1868 Japan has marked historical time by imperial reigns. When the emperor changes, so does the calendar, and when the emperor dies, he takes the name of the era with him. Hirohito ascended the throne in 1926, beginning the Shōwa era. The reign-name Shōwa had been chosen for its auspicious meaning: at home, enlightened government; abroad, world peace. The era ended in 1989 when Hirohito died, and after his death he became known as the Shōwa emperor. But since his long reign had brought neither enlightment nor peace, it immediately received a new name in Japanese memory. Looking back on its more than sixty years—which included economic depression, right-wing terrorism, aggressive war, unconditional defeat, foreign occupation, democratic reform, stable peace, unprecedented prosperity, and the rise to world power—Japanese called it "turbulent Shōwa."

The phrase stuck, an instant cliché that, like most clichés, told a simple truth. Whatever their position, Japanese agreed that the age of Hirohito had been turbulent. Hirohito himself had long thought so. But once he and his era were gone, there was a rush to remembrance. During the emperor's seemingly interminable terminal illness in late 1988, the media had prepared for X-day, their code name for the day of the imperial demise. When it came, in January 1989, the blitz of media history was complete. Yet the flood of memory swirled from deeper sources than television. It was as if a dam had broken on thoughts long held but seldom spoken.

Less than a week after the emperor died, polls revealed that one quarter of the Japanese people believed that Hirohito, too, bore "war responsibility." Such matter-of-factness was said to have finally broken the "chrysanthemum taboo" on straight talk about the Shōwa emperor's role in World War II. New documents began to tumble into print, diaries of ministers and palace chamberlains, even a "soliloquy" recording the words of the emperor himself about his actions during the war. Now that the era had ended, it was possible for the first time to write Shōwa history whole. For many people, among them the author of this book, it was also necessary to write its history anew, with particular concern for the more than nominal link between "Shōwa History and the Emperor"—the title of this book when it appeared in Japanese in 1991. They often wrote, like Professor Irokawa, in a white heat that fused history and memory, not for the sake of posterity but for themselves.

For this is a profoundly personal book. In this aspect, too, it is linked to the outpouring of recollections that appeared after the emperor's death. Because Japanese born since 1926—the majority of the population—had known no other era, remembering Shōwa meant retelling their own life stories. In reminiscences with titles like "My Shōwa," people began to sort out the intertwining of their personal pasts with the larger national history of war and peace, privation and prosperity. Mostly they recalled private experiences, from foraging for food during the war to conserving electricity after the price of oil rose in the early 1970s. Neither the emperor nor the state figured prominently in their accounts; they lived their lives "on the ground." Yet it was clear that those lives had been profoundly affected by the high history of Shōwa, even though it seemed to have been conducted without great regard for its impact upon them.

This is Professor Irokawa's subject: "the emperor and the people," he often calls it, evoking the larger question of how history happens in modern Japan. In Shōwa terms, how did the state, epitomized in the emperor, manage to run things the way it did, and how did "ordinary Japanese" let themselves be run that way? For Irokawa and others of his generation, this is both a historical question and a personal matter. He describes it as "contemporary history," which in Japanese literally means "history of the same period" one is living in. In an earlier version of same-period history written in Shōwa 50 (1975), Irokawa had called it "self-history."* Such personal history, he argued, worked as an antidote to national history, which chronicled the state and ignored the experience of the people. In *The Age of Hirohito* he brings the two together, telling the national story of Shōwa from a personal point of view.

And what is his point of view? R. G. Collingwood once described the historian in ancient Greece as an "autobiographer of his generation," whose subject chose him rather than the other way around. Born in 1925,

---

*Irokawa Daikichi, *Aru Shōwashi: jibunshi no kokoromi* [a history of Shōwa; an attempt at a self-history] (Tokyo; Chūō kōronsha, 1975). The book sold over 100,000 copies.

Irokawa belongs to what is sometimes called the "wartime generation," which refers to those Japanese who came of age between the beginning of the China War in 1937 and the defeat in 1945. In their teens and early twenties, they were too young to have experienced the prewar years, old enough to have been captured by wartime chauvinism (often in middle school), and young enough to feel betrayed by the state and its surrender. The subject that chose them was war. From their ranks came some of the most ardent champions of postwar democracy, progressives dedicated to rooting out the structures of the imperial past that had brought Japan to aggression and catastrophe.

Partly because many of their elders were killed during the war and partly because they were so vocal and full of hope for the postwar future, this compressed generation rose to prominence soon after the war and remained the intellectual leaders of the progressives for decades afterward. Irokawa Daikichi, now seventy, is among its older members, the writer Ōe Kenzaburō, born in 1935, among the youngest. Irokawa was mobilized from Tokyo University into the Navy in 1944, and in 1993 he wrote a book in remembrance of his fellow students who had died in the war.* Ōe, a child during the war, wrote his first famous short story, "The Catch" (1958), about how war brought tragedy to his village, and he has remained committed to anti-nuclear and anti-war causes to this day. The wartime generation, in effect, were the youth so affected by the war that it changed the way they saw the world.

The issue that most haunted them was the submissiveness of the people to the dictates of the imperial state. Hence their concern with the emperor and the people who revered and followed him—people like themselves and their families—and their fear that genuine democracy had eluded postwar Japan, undermined both by continuities from the prewar past and changes caused by the present prosperity. As progressives, their views ranged across a broad spectrum of the Left, the dominant position among intellectuals from the end of the war until the 1970s. Steadfast critics of the postwar status quo, figures like Irokawa shouldered the burden of Shōwa in a double way. They were representatives of the generation old enough to have experienced the war—and Hirohito as the divine generalissimo on the white horse. And they were also progressives whose hopes for upending history were undone by patterns from the past—Hirohito as

---

Wadatsumi no tomo e [To the friends of the sea] (Tokyo: Iwanami Shoten, 1993). Founded in 1949 in memory of the students lost in the war (the voices from the sea), the Wadatsumi Society has dedicated itself to antiwar and related activities.

the gentle biologist and family man, now constitutionally declared a sym-bol-emperor, but still emperor nonetheless. No wonder they took both era and emperor personally.

In fact, this generation produced much of the remembering of Shōwa that overflowed after the emperor's death. Whatever their political views, this was their age, their emperor, and they could not but identify with it and with him. As the author admits toward the end of this book, the younger people born since the war (the so-called postwar generations) do not care much about the emperor one way or the other. Having no direct wartime complicity, they are not beset by doubts about the emperor's war responsibility.

Indeed, it was only since Hirohito's death—and the end of the Cold War, which coincidentally occurred in the same year—that the wider pub-lic finally began to confront larger questions of war responsibility. The ex-perience of the "comfort women," the Asians dragooned into serving the Japanese Army as prostitutes during the war, so long denied by the gov-ernment, became a matter of public record, mentioned, if briefly, in school textbooks. The biological experiments committed by the infamous Unit 731 of the Japanese army were exhibited in town halls and on television. Nationalists and conservatives vigorously opposed dwelling on the nasti-ness of the national past and continued their efforts to whitewash Japan's aggression. Yet the fiftieth anniversary of the end of the war in 1995 saw a wider debate about war responsibility than anyone might have foreseen at the time that "the age of Hirohito" passed into history in 1989.

The war and the emperor are not the whole story of Shōwa as the author tells it here. He is also in search of larger quarry, what the English subtitle calls "modern Japan." An accomplished historian, Professor Irokawa is well known to Japanese audiences as an avid practitioner of "people's his-tory." His aversion to the imperial state, acquired firsthand during the war, led him to seek alternative sources of political energy in Japan's past. In the villages of nineteenth-century Japan he found forms of local community that were economically progressive, politically creative, and socially egali-tarian enough to seem to him almost protodemocratic. In his work on the Meiji era (1868–1912)—the first reign of the new modern state under Hi-rohito's grandfather, the Meiji emperor—Irokawa located popular sources of democratic politics in the Freedom and People's Rights Movement of the 1870s and 1880s. In a dramatic discovery, which has since been recreated in Japanese and even in American television documentaries, he unearthed from an old storehouse in a village outside Tokyo a draft constitution written by grass-roots activists in the movement.* But their progressive views did not prevail, and the imperial state established its authoritarian structure in 1890 at the expense of democratic government.

True democracy, the author felt, must come from the people, "from below," and not be imposed by the state. Many agreed with him, the more so considering that the institutions of Japan's postwar democracy had come from above, established under the occupation by a constitution written by Americans. Irokawa not only wrote people's history; he practiced people's politics. Like many progressive intellectuals, he committed himself to a range of causes to defend democracy against the state, from the anti-security-treaty protests of 1960 through the citizens' movements against pollution in the 1970s to his founding of the "Is this as good as Japan can be?" Citizens League in 1980. Irokawa announced the disbanding of the League in August 1994, admitting that his hopes for democracy remained unfulfilled. At the same time he declared his intention to work on behalf of the Minamata pollution victims during the fortieth anniversary of their affliction, in 1995.

Irokawa's hopes for democracy, frequently dashed but not demolished, animate his search for modern Japan. He weaves a people's history through his account of Shōwa, alternately idealizing the "ordinary Japanese" for surviving the excesses of the state and chastising them for submitting to its demands. He is far more critical of the "life-style revolution" of consumer capitalism and high-growth economics than most of the "ordinary Japanese" he invokes. But he is also far fiercer than they are in protesting the costs of growth and the social inequities that beset women and minorities in Japanese society. Like the ordinary Japanese, he has little use for politics as the government practices it. Although this book was written before the fall in 1993 of the Liberal Democratic Party after thirty-eight years in power, the author's call for "fundamental restructuring of the political parties" remains unanswered. Despite the proliferation of new parties with new names, from his point of view they all espouse the same old politics, which is not the politics of the people. Irokawa also shares with the vast majority of ordinary Japanese a belief in Japan's "peace constitution," a belief that is itself a product of Shōwa and the war. But he would have Japan extend its ideal among its Asian neighbors and spread the message

---

*Irokawa Daikichi, *The Culture of the Meiji Period* (Princeton: Princeton University Press, 1985). For the video documentary, *The Pacific Century*, Part 3, "Meiji: Asia's Challenge to the West" (1992), contact the Annenberg/CPB Project, Burlington, VT.

of peace abroad, rather than walling up its pacifism within its island
borders.

For American readers, well supplied as we are with stereotypes about
Japan, Irokawa Daikichi offers a voice that is both critical of Japanese society and also deeply committed to the possibility of change for the better.
As a historian he knows that vast changes have taken place over the course
of Japan's modern history. As someone who lived through "turbulent
Shōwa," he knows that constancy of criticism is the most important civic
virtue. Criticism in the service of change: as a guide for "facing the twenty-
first century," it makes good sense for all of us.

Carol Gluck

PREFACE TO THE
ENGLISH EDITION

I n Japan, the fiftieth anniversary of the end of the Second World War
has brought a wave of popular interest in history. Along with a renewed
debate over the meaning of the war, people are taking a closer look at
the past half-century, when Japan recovered from painful defeat to become
one of the world's leading economic powers. The current wave of interest
in history is accompanied by an unprecedented amount of reflection and
examination of Japan's recent past. Also, in the wake of the Japan-centered
public discussion of the war and the emperor's role in it, which arose after
Emperor Hirohito's death in 1989, there is now a desire to see our past not
only as Japanese history but also in the context of Japan's relationships
with Asia and the West.

This broadening of focus has come about in a period of transition for
Japan, and it is partly a result of the changes in Japan's relationships with
its neighbors since Hirohito's death. The establishment of an Asia-Pacific
economic bloc free from Western control and the continuing, rapid growth
of the Chinese economy are forcing Japan to make fundamental changes in
its priorities and policies. Until now, the Japanese government and business
community had considered ties to America to be of primary importance,
and believed it imperative for foreign relations to follow the leadership of
Washington. Recently, however, Japan has begun to strengthen ties with
Asia. This gradual shift away from an America-centered approach to international affairs appears likely to become more pronounced in the future.

Nevertheless, a certain dissonance remains, for, even though Japan is
turning its attention to its own neighborhood, its leaders are still en-
meshed in the old mindset of venerating America and denigrating Asia.
Last year a cabinet minister asserted that the Southeast Asian economies
are developing rapidly because Japan liberated these countries from Western control in World War II. Though he was forced to resign, there are
many conservative politicians who, like him, still refer to the "Greater East

Asia War" of liberation and self-defense, and refuse to acknowledge Japan's responsibility as an aggressor. They maintain that Japan was falsely convicted of crimes against humanity and peace at the Tokyo War Crimes Trial in 1948—and that this conviction was a form of victor's justice imposed on a humiliated Japan.

Through the years, Japan's political leaders have taken any available opportunity to express their rejection of the war crimes trial verdict. Among many such outbursts was that of Education Minister Fujio Masayuki, who, in 1986, indicated that he accepted pro forma the decision of the trial's International Military Tribunal, but in reality rejected its validity. Such "slips of the tongue" were not denied by Prime Minister Nakasone Yasuhiro (who later asked Fujio to resign). Indeed, Nakasone's view was little different—he was the first prime minister to flout the trial's indictment of class-A war criminals by making an official visit to Yasukuni Shrine, where their spirits are honored, on August 15, 1985, the fortieth anniversary of the end of the war.

As the fiftieth anniversary approached, these slips of the tongue began to occur with greater frequency. In May 1994, Justice Minister Nagano Shigeto, serving in the cabinet of Hata Tsutomu, said, "I believe the story of the Nanjing massacre is a fabrication. It is wrong to call the war a war of aggression; it was a war of self-defense, a sincere effort to liberate the colonies and establish the Greater East Asian Co-prosperity Sphere." When his remarks were criticized vehemently throughout Asia, he, too, was forced to resign.

Three months later Sakurai Shin, the Director General of the Environment Agency, expressed similar sentiments and was forced to resign following a heated protest from the Republic of Korea. Then, in October, Hashimoto Ryūtarō, Minister of International Trade and Industry in the cabinet of Murayama Tomiichi and a candidate to become the next prime minister, stated in the Diet, "There are aspects that [China and Korea] could regard as aggression by Japan," but added, "I question whether Japan's war with the Western nations can be defined as a war of aggression." Japan's neighbors condemned this statement as an attempt to mask Japan's past aggressions in Asia. But Hashimoto did not resign—indeed, Prime Minister Murayama (a socialist, no less) defended him.

These three comments coming from Japanese cabinet ministers within the space of a year must certainly have put the peoples of Asia on guard. Then, during his 1994 trip to Asia, Hosokawa Morihiro became the first prime minister ever to state frankly that Japan had engaged in a war of aggression. The Asian nations welcomed this expression of regret and assumption of moral responsibility. But when Hosokawa returned to Japan he was confronted with opposition from his own cabinet and toned down his remarks, admitting only that "there were some aggressive actions." The official Japanese position thus returned to the ambiguity that has been a constant during the past half-century. Even fifty years after the war, the Japanese government found it difficult to admit that the war Japan initiated and fought from 1931 to 1945 was a war of aggression, and continued to resist admitting that Japan as a nation bears the responsibility for the war.

The roots of this tenacious attitude among Japan's leaders can be traced to the American postwar occupation of Japan. An initially liberal occupation policy reversed course with the advent of the Cold War, as the United States set out to use Japan as a bulwark against communism. The occupation authorities allowed conservative nationalists, purged for their wartime activities, to return to public office and discontinued the investigation of the conservatives' responsibility for the war. The American authorities also opposed bringing the emperor, the person most responsible for the war, before the Tokyo War Crimes Tribunal and absolved him of responsibility. This encouraged the conservatives in the government and reinforced their belief that the emperor was not responsible for the war. Unfortunately, until now, most of us ordinary Japanese did not have the power to take up the issue of the emperor's war responsibility.

With the fiftieth anniversary of the end of the war, questions of responsibility will finally be extensively debated. I hope that this kind of discussion will confront the history of the Shōwa Era (1926–1989) head-on. Indeed, a closer examination of Japanese history during Hirohito's reign reveals that the emperor's responsibility is irrefutable. That is a focus of this book.

In conclusion I would like to pay my deepest respect to Professor Mikiso Hane and John Urda for their efforts in undertaking the difficult task of translating the original Japanese text into English. I also wish to express my deepest gratitude to Professor Carol Gluck, who worked tirelessly to bring this project to fruition and has written the Foreword, as well as to Bruce K. Nichols, for devoting his time and effort to facilitating the publication of this edition.

Daikichi Irokawa
Tokyo
1995

THE
AGE OF
HIROHITO

Introduction

THE LIMITS OF CONTEMPORARY HISTORY

W hen I entered Tokyo University in the fall of 1943, contemporary history was not recognized as a subject for study. According to my professors in the history department, events after the
Meiji Restoration of 1868 were "not appropriate" for scholarly investigation. The interpretation of recent events, they felt, was not only subject to
frequent revision with the continuing discovery of new documents but
also was plagued by the subjectivity of historians who had lived through
or even participated in those events. In other words, contemporary, or
modern, history was seen as not sufficiently objective.

Needless to say, the study of history is not merely the listing of objective facts. History is rewritten constantly. For example, it is said that the
Meiji emperor (1852–1912) and the Shōwa emperor (1903–1989) kept
records of their reigns. The Shōwa emperor was especially alert and active,
so it seems likely that he kept a number of written accounts; and, indeed,
it appears that there are diaries from his youth. None of these writings
have yet been made public. General Douglas MacArthur, who ruled Japan
for some 2,000 days, met with the emperor eleven times. The records of
these meetings have not been made public. It is known, however, that
memos and stenographic notes were made (portions of which have been
leaked) and supposedly are stored somewhere in the Foreign Ministry and
in the Imperial Household Ministry.

Until these materials are made public, a historical discussion of the politics or foreign affairs of the occupation period remains problematic. With
this caveat, I shall interpret the events of the period.

The Shōwa era lasted sixty-two years, from the end of 1926 until the
beginning of 1989. Although any number of major issues can be discussed
within this time frame, I have chosen three main themes. The first theme,
"War and Peace," runs through the Shōwa era. Though historians usually
bisect the era into a period of war and another of peace (demarcated on

August 15, 1945, the date of Japan's surrender), this view is an oversim-
plification. Peace was found during the war years, at least in the lifestyles
of most people, and the postwar period was not a time of unbroken calm.
The second theme presented here is another enormous topic: the
"Lifestyle Revolution." During the Shōwa period, an essentially agrarian
society underwent fundamental changes. The modern urban lifestyle
that prevails in Japan today first appeared in the 1920s and, despite a
brief disruption during the war and the immediate postwar period, the
tempo of modernization increased very quickly after 1945 and seemed
to reach its upper limits by the 1980s.

My third and most important theme is "The Emperor and the People."
If the emperor system had disappeared after the 1945 defeat, this discussion, of course, would not be necessary. But the emperor and the government leaders somehow came through untouched and untainted by their
responsibility for the war. Although the essential character of the emperor
system underwent major changes, the system survived. Today it has become an extremely stable institution. But when we examine the relationship between the emperor and the people—a part of Japanese society that
the world does not see—many problems become visible: problems of ideology, education, relations with neighboring countries, Japan's constitution, and so on.

By focusing on these three themes—war and peace, the lifestyle revolution, and the emperor and the people—I hope to present a basic understanding of the Shōwa period. I then close with a reflection on what Japan
has achieved, what it has failed to achieve, and what remains for Japan in
the twenty-first century.

Chapter 1

WAR AND PEACE

FROM THE PERSPECTIVE OF THE VICTIMS OF WAR

During the Shōwa era (1926–1989), Japanese society underwent a rapid transformation: people's lifestyles changed completely. Even the lifestyle changes wrought by the Meiji Restoration of 1868 cannot compare. Even though the Meiji Restoration involved the transformation from a feudal to a modern capitalist society, the lives of ordinary people did not change significantly.

In contrast, the changes people experienced during the Shōwa years were truly momentous. Shortly after the Shōwa era began, the army made its first expedition into China's Shandong province and, in 1927, Japan was plunged into a series of conflicts leading to the period of "total war," from 1937 to 1945. Approximately 10 million Japanese men (out of a total Japanese population of about 70 million) were sent to fight on the Asian continent and the Aleutian and South Pacific islands. The number of victims in these lands invaded by the Japanese forces was many times greater than the number of Japanese dead and wounded.

In Japan, the people underwent total mobilization, which shook their ways of life at the roots. These first twenty years of the Shōwa era were thus a time of extraordinary change. Ultimately, all those living in Japan, including Koreans and Taiwanese, were drawn into the war in one way or another: not a single person lived through those years untouched by the conflict. Some were pursued by gunfire in foreign lands, some fell in battle, but most Japanese experienced great hardships at home. Toward the end of the war, they endured air raids, saw their houses burned to the ground, had to send their children away from home, and lost family members. The war was not limited to the military or diplomatic arenas, but was a momentous event in the lives of everyone in Japan. All Japanese, without exception, were affected not only by the war, which threatened their lives, but by the overwhelming changes in life brought about by modernization in the postwar years. But the women, without question, suffered the most.

Women suffered from many different burdens during this period. Mothers, wives, and daughters endured the hardship of supporting the people who went to the battlefields, but many also served in the public sector. Close to 2 million women, including housewives, were mobilized as factory laborers, and even young girls were organized into volunteer corps to produce war goods. In addition, women were responsible for all the housework necessary to support working men and schoolchildren. They thus undertook strenuous physical labor without compensation during a time of material shortages. It is often assumed that the hardships and sacrifices endured by women were the same as those borne by ordinary workers and tenant farmers, but this perception is mistaken. Even though all were laborers, when the men returned home they often behaved like tyrants. If male workers were slaves of the capitalists, the women were the slaves of the slaves.

Despite their difficult situation, toward the end of the war women—exactly like men—were rounded up to work in the factories to produce goods for the war effort and were used as auxiliary combatants during air raids. The women who underwent these experiences emerged tougher and highly disciplined. Their harsh wartime experiences helped Japanese women become aware of their right to a new status in the postwar period.

Most Japanese assume that American culture arrived with the U.S. occupation forces in the postwar years. However, Japan was already inundated with American culture at the end of the Taishō (1912–1926) and the beginning of the Shōwa eras, as the nation rebuilt from the devastation of the Great Kantō Earthquake of September 1, 1923, which destroyed sixty-three percent of houses in Tokyo and killed more than 104,000 people.

At that time, the United States was in the midst of a cultural boom. Most Americans had begun to own cars in the 1920s, preceding Japan by some forty years. American streets were jammed with automobiles, and some 50,000 people—an incredible number—died in auto accidents during that decade. Automation had already arrived in American factories and, as so many Japanese saw in the Chaplin film *Modern Times*, assembly line manufacturing had been adopted. Labor rights activists, anarchists, communists, and feminists had all appeared in the United States. It was a dynamic era.

The cinema, then at the center of American culture, was greeted with open arms in Japan, and Japanese directors showed off their American influences. This was the age of the *moga* and *mobo,* the "modern girls" and "modern boys" who embraced Western fashions, attitudes, and lifestyles. After the Great Kantō Earthquake, new buildings lined the streets, and more women began to appear in the job market, though primarily at lower-level positions.

Though modern culture was present in Japan in the early Shōwa years, it was not widespread. One reason for its limited impact was the rigid social structure of Japan in those years, but the main reason was the worldwide Great Depression and the outbreak of war.

Life During the Great Depression

When the Great Depression came to Japan in 1929, the infatuation with modern Western culture dissipated immediately. Labor disputes, tenancy disputes, unemployment, and the plight of the poor all came to the fore, triggered by a bank crisis and the wave of bankruptcies that struck small and medium-sized businesses. During 1929 and 1930, about fifty percent of these businesses went into bankruptcy, and some factories were forced to close down.

In the villages, prices of farm products tumbled, in some cases more than half, creating desperate conditions on the land. Large numbers of farmers who could find no way to survive in Japan emigrated to Brazil and Argentina. Many people also emigrated to Manchuria in search of land and a better life. Ishikawa Tatsuzō, one of Japan's leading novelists at the time, wrote about these emigrants in his novel *Sōbō (The Common People),* which won the first Akutagawa Prize in 1935.

When the Depression hit the rural areas in 1930, Hani Motoko (1873–1957), a contributor to the women's magazine *Fujin no Tomo (Woman's Friend),* labored desperately to stem the drastic decline of the farm villages. Along with graduates of the school she founded, the Jiyū Gakuen (the Free School, an experimental academy for girls), she organized *tomo no kai* (benevolent associations) throughout Japan to help people change their lives to adapt to the impact of the Depression. Helping people find ways to get by with less was a noble aim, but people who had nothing to begin with could not manage on less. Despite their good intentions, the *tomo no kai* had only a minimal effect. The situation was especially severe in the northeast, where Miyazawa Kenji (1896–1933, a poet and writer of children's stories) depicted the grim scene in poems and photographs taken before he died in 1933.

Statistics from the Depression era also indicate the conditions that prevailed during those years. The ten-volume *Senzen Nihon Shakai Jigyō Chōsa Shiryō-shūsei* presents documents collected by the Home Ministry and data gathered by independent organizations from 1930 to 1941.* Of this massive collection, volumes 1 to 3, entitled *Poverty,* include reports of the horrible conditions afflicting people at the bottom levels of Japanese society. Volume 4 discusses *Vagrants.* Volume 5, *Protection of Children,* deals with the problem of aiding the children from poor families who had been sold and were living like slaves. Volume 6 is *Mothers and Children,* and volume 7, *The Elderly.*

The volumes provide shocking statistics on the number of farmers who, with nothing more to sell, were forced to sell their daughters. In the hard-hit six prefectures of northeastern Japan, the number of women sold jumped almost five times—from 12,180 to 58,173 in the two-year period from 1932 to 1934. The period from 1931 to 1937 was when conditions were grimmest in the northeastern farm villages. The numbers tell the story: the region produced 2,196 geisha, 4,421 brothel inmates, some 6,000 *sake* servers, and more than 3,200 waitresses. The *sake* servers and waitresses were, in fact, forced to prostitute themselves. The number of men who bought the services of these women probably totaled several million.

Though the practice no longer prevails, before the war an average of 200,000 young girls were sold annually to serve as maids and nursemaids—a number exceeding the 179,000 women who became factory workers each year. Maids and nursemaids received one cotton kimono, one pair of wooden clogs, and two or three yen during special holidays like the late-summer *bon* festivals and the New Year celebrations. The rest of the year, they worked for nothing. This situation was prevalent throughout Japan until 1937 or 1938. After the Second World War, the number of maids decreased as the demand for war-related labor brought women into the munitions factories.

These figures show where the hardships and sufferings were felt most deeply during the Shōwa economic crisis. Because of such conditions at the lower levels of society, the military could take advantage of the unem-

Senzen Nihon Shakai Jigyō Chōsa Shiryō-shūsei (Collection of Documents on Surveys of Prewar Japanese Social Work), edited by Ichibangas Yasuko (Tokyo: Keisō Shobō, 1983).

ployed, impoverished youth and the spiritually exhausted Japanese people to wage its aggressive adventures on the Asian continent. The move to expand the empire also appealed to the struggling financial community, which hoped new markets on the continent would end the Depression, and to an ambitious group of politicians who aspired to a stronger power base.

This perspective on the causes of Japanese expansionism differs from the conventional view that a small number of military men with a carefully formulated plan of aggression dragged the people and the state along unwillingly. Instead, the militarist forces emerged from the terrible conditions plaguing the people during the Depression and used that opportunity to turn the nation toward aggression on the continent and war.

ESCAPE FROM THE WORLD ECONOMIC CRISIS

Raising the Curtain on a Dark Era

When Crown Prince Hirohito—the eldest son of Yoshihito, reigning emperor of the Taishō era—returned from his studies in England in 1921, he was very liberal, convinced of the advantages of a free and open lifestyle.* He played golf in the imperial compounds, went skiing, and went out to the Ginza to drink beer with his friends from the Peers' School. But, as his younger brother Prince Mikasa once noted, his life entirely changed after the Toranomon Incident.

As soon as Prince Hirohito became regent for the ailing Taishō emperor, Yoshihito, he was nearly killed in an assassination attempt. Known as the Toranomon Incident after the section of Tokyo where it occurred, the attack took place on December 27, 1923. In the chaos following the devastating Great Kantō Earthquake, rumors quickly spread that foreigners and radicals were setting fires, looting, and plotting to seize power. Mobs beat or killed anyone suspected of being Korean, Chinese, or leftist. With some police and army complicity, these mobs targeted the poorer

---

*Since 1868 it has been customary to assign a special name to each new reign. The era of Mutsuhito's rule (1868–1912) was named the Meiji; during his lifetime Mutsuhito was known by the title Kinjō (currently above, meaning reigning) Tennō (emperor), but upon his death he was referred to as Emperor Meiji. His oldest son Yoshihito held the throne from 1912 to 1926, the Taishō era, and upon his death he was referred to as Emperor Taishō. When his oldest son Hirohito took the throne, the era name adopted was Shōwa (enlightened harmony), and since his death in 1989 he is referred to as Emperor Shōwa.

wards in Tokyo and murdered common people as well as prominent anarchists like Ōsugi Sakae and his wife Itō Noe. Thousands of Koreans, Chinese, and leftists in the Tokyo area were massacred. To avenge these actions, Nanba Taisuke, the radical son of a conservative Diet member, fired a shot at Regent Hirohito—then the most prominent representative of the emperor system—just a month before he was to marry Princess Kuninomiya Nagako.

The Toranomon Incident brought down Prime Minister Yamamoto Gonnohyōe's cabinet, but the new government under Kiyoura Keigo soon fell to intraparty squabbling. The Shōwa era started from this dark point in history—an extremely inauspicious beginning for the mild-tempered Hirohito. Suddenly the young regent was placed under strict supervision by the court of officials and no longer was able to behave as he pleased. The Toranomon Incident was thus an ominous turning point for the imperial court. Crown Prince Hirohito, who had returned from Europe imbued with the ideals of freedom, had to return to the life of a caged bird, far removed from ordinary life.

In 1925, more pervasive restrictions took effect with the enactment of the Peace Preservation Law. This law, which strictly limited basic human rights such as freedom of speech, freedom of thought, and freedom of assembly, was intended to counter the impact of the recently adopted universal male suffrage act. Regent Hirohito was not directly responsible for this law, of course, but laws could be enforced only after the emperor (in this instance, the regent as proxy for the ailing Taishō emperor) had signed them. The repressive measures this law allowed had grave consequences.

As 1926 closed, the Regent Hirohito became the emperor, marking the formal beginning of the Shōwa era, which lasted for sixty-two years and two weeks. Financial panic broke out in 1927, and a run on banks soon spread throughout Japan, plunging the nation into gloom. On July 24 of the same year, one of Japan's foremost novelists, Akutagawa Ryūnosuke, committed suicide.* His note read, "I feel a vague sense of anxiety. . . . During the past two years I have continuously thought only about dying." Then the following September, Tokutomi Roka, another well-known and much-loved writer, died of an illness.† Other events, most

---

*A number of Akutagawa's (1892–1927) stories, such as *Hell Screen*, *Kappa*, and *Rashōmon*, have been translated into English.

†Tokutomi Roka's (1868–1927) *Footprints in the Snow* has been translated into English. His most famous work is *Hototogisu* (Cuckoo).

notably the Manchurian Incident, continued to intensify the dark mood.

On September 18, 1931, officers of Japan's Kwantung Army (named after the province in Manchuria where it was initially stationed) acting on their own, set off the Manchurian Incident. These officers acted out of their frustration with the Japanese government which, in 1930, had bent to worldwide pressure and signed the London naval arms limitation treaty reducing the number of warships. The signing later led some young naval officers to attempt a coup on May 15, 1932, the so-called May 15th Incident in which Prime Minister Inukai Tsuyoshi was assassinated.

Like the earlier bombing of Zhang Zuolin's railway car on the South Manchurian railroad in June 1928, the subsequent invasion of Manchuria in 1931 was not simply part of a plot hatched by officers of the Kwantung Army. The Army General Staff and the head of the First General Staff Division had foreknowledge of the officers' intentions. Moreover, the supreme commander of the Korean expeditionary force, General Hayashi Senjūrō, knew of the plan; as soon as he received a wire from the supreme commander of the Kwantung Army, he immediately dispatched bomber planes from Korea to hit targets in Manchuria. Then, without the approval of the army's commander-in-chief—the emperor—he sent the 4,000-man First Brigade across the Korean border into Manchuria.

The death of Zhang Zuolin, a Manchurian warlord, had prepared the groundwork for Japan's takeover of Manchuria (that is, all of northeastern China). The invasion plan was carefully worked out by Lieutenant Colonel Ishiwara Kanji, the chief of staff of the Kwantung Army, and his colleagues, and we now know that the plan had been sent to the emperor. The authorities may not have expected the plan to be put into effect so soon, but they nonetheless should be considered coconspirators."*

1933: Year of Destiny

The eighth year of Shōwa (1933) saw the birth of the Crown Prince, Akihito, Japan's current emperor. This long-awaited event was greeted by joyous shouts of *"Banzai, banzai!"* from the Japanese people. But 1933 also marked a dark turning point in Japanese—and world—history: Japan's unilateral withdrawal from the League of Nations and the rise of Nazi

*See Kantōgun, "Manshū Jihen Kimitsu Seiryaku Nisshi," *Manshū Jihenshi Daigo kan-an*, Sanbo Honbu (Kwantung Army, "Journal of the Secret Policy Concerning the Manchurian Incident," in *History of the Manchurian Incident*, vol. 5, General Staff Headquarters.)

Germany. Though Japan, regarded by many as "the orphan of the world," acted alone in withdrawing from the league, Germany was not far behind. In 1933, Hitler seized power and Nazi Germany, which was soon to batter the world, was born. In the same year, the United States adopted the New Deal program to cut through the Great Depression.

The choices made by Germany and the United States present a striking contrast. Two to three years after Hitler took power he declared his decision to rearm and introduced his policy of expansion into neighboring countries. He annexed Austria, then Czechoslovakia, and soon extended his reach into Poland. He sought to resolve the economic and social discontent of the German people by turning outward and expanding German territory.

In contrast, the United States turned inward. It largely ignored the world and instead, concentrated on rebuilding its domestic economy. A huge amount of the nation's resources was invested in the undeveloped western and central regions in order to stimulate domestic demand. Decisive action was taken, such as the Agricultural Adjustment Act to assist suffering farmers, the Tennessee Valley Authority development project, and joint ventures by public and private organizations to assist the massive numbers of unemployed. Though the Soviet Union regarded both the United States and Germany as imperialist powers, there were profound differences between the two nations. However, Japanese policy makers of that time were unable to discern these differences.

Considering the situation in Japan at this time casts the Manchurian Incident in a new light. Two years before the Great Depression, Japan was already plagued by financial crisis. When the global financial collapse swept across Japan and its economic world, rural and urban life fell into chaos. Japan's leaders groped for ways to cut through the difficulties and gradually formed three general groups with different solutions to the hardships.

The first possible route was the "Shōwa Restoration" advocated by radical nationalists and military officers. This course entailed forcefully breaking out of the political and economic crisis by temporarily suspending the parliamentary system and concentrating political power in the hands of the emperor (thereby restoring the "proper" relationship between the emperor and the people). Advocates of this right-wing movement called for equality under the emperor, a "Shōwa Revolution" aimed at redistributing some of the enormous wealth concentrated in the financial sector. But this faction's real motive was military: the creation of a colonial empire in Manchuria and other areas of the continent through military force.

The left, on the other hand, advocated a popular revolution to overcome the economic crisis. They hoped that concentrating power in the hands of the workers and peasants would change the capitalist system from the roots up. The left believed that the country's difficulties could be resolved only by abandoning the emperor system and turning over state power to the people.

These two opposing factions beneath Japan's efforts to break free of the Depression in the early years of Shōwa spurred class conflicts and violent clashes. In retrospect, neither of these two approaches could have succeeded. The actual course of history settled on the path chosen by a third group.

By cleverly making use of right-wing power in the military and political arenas but keeping a safe distance from the extreme rightists, a group of pragmatic military officers known as the Tōseiha (control faction) and government bureaucrats linked with the new and old *zaibatsu* (family-based conglomerates) then seeking to make the Asian continent their base of operations. This faction set out to free Japan from economic depression by pursuing a course of aggression.

To further their objectives, they assassinated Zhang Zuolin, and in the same year imprisoned several thousand communists and labor leaders. Following these successes, they systematically provoked military clashes along the route of the South Manchurian Railway, which was under the control of the Kwantung Army. They used these confrontations to bring all of Manchuria under Japanese control. Then, with Manchuria as a base, the military slowly infiltrated what is now Inner Mongolia and entered northern China, in places like Rehe Province. Though these actions were taken by the military, it did not act alone; the policy was enthusiastically supported by segments of the conservative parties, the newly risen conglomerates, and the new bureaucrats.

If the emperor had intended to push for peace or pursue a British-style constitutional government, he could have unequivocally expressed his views on the proper route out of the Depression. The emperor at that time was a supreme authority with sovereign power over the entire Japanese imperial state—a status totally different from that of the symbolic emperor now. Although under the constitution the emperor had to have the cabinet's consent to exercise his political authority, he had sole authority over armed forces as their supreme commander. If, as Hirohito later stated, he had desired to be a constitutional, peace-loving monarch at that time, he should have taken a stand by 1933, when the aggression was beginning in earnest. Soon after it became extremely difficult to take any action against the militarists.

Japan's formal withdrawal from the League of Nations in March of 1933 was the first step toward aggression on the continent, the course favored by the increasingly dominant Tōseiha. The withdrawal also meant that Japan would proceed in unison with Hitler, who had just seized power and was poised to annex Germany's neighboring nations. In Japan, only a few believed that the Depression could be overcome by a policy of international cooperation based on friendly relations with England and the United States and by investing the nation's resources in underdeveloped areas like the northern island of Hokkaidō, the northwestern and southwestern regions along the Japan Sea, the southern island of Kyūshū, and the colonies. Those who favored a large-scale New Deal-like program to increase domestic demand and boost the nation's economy lacked powerful backing. Their moderate ideas were overwhelmed by the radical views of the left and right and disappeared without ever having a chance to succeed.

Abandoning its policy of international cooperation by withdrawing from the League of Nations inevitably led Japan to renounce the Washington and London arms limitation treaties. The crucial steps toward war came in the form of two blows against the constitutional parliamentary government, which had survived for a decade and a half. These two violent episodes are now known by their dates: the so-called May 15th and February 26th incidents.

The system of party government in Japan ended, strictly speaking, with the assassination of Prime Minister Inukai Tsuyoshi, the head of the Seiyūkai party, on May 15, 1932—the May 15th Incident. Inukai's death ended the constitutional practice of having the head of the majority political party in the Diet form a cabinet in accordance with the will of the people. Almost all subsequent prime ministers came from the military—generals or admirals—not from the majority political party.

The May 15th Incident was a blow to party government, but the death knell was struck by the attempted coup of February 26, 1936, in which radical military officers assassinated a number of key government officials. Thereafter, the political parties could no longer use constitutional principles to exert influence. The rise of the aristocratic Prime Minister Konoe Fumimaro (who held office from 1937 to 1939 and from 1940 to 1941), provided a faint glimmer of hope for parliamentary restoration, but he owed his political life to the absolute support of the navy and army and thus did not really represent the political parties in the Diet.

The military planned many other coups between May 15, 1932, and February 26, 1936, but these attempts did not materialize, partly because of internal power struggles in the military. And as constitutional government weakened, the Japanese state rapidly changed direction toward the right-wing plan of expansion on the continent. The emperor was angered by the military's usurpation of authority in the February 26th Incident, and he castigated the commander general of military law, but Hirohito's angry outburst came too late.

Even though the emperor spoke like a constitutional monarch, the political parties, which were the foundation of his authority, had already been crippled. He no longer had the power to control the military and assume political authority, and the question of whether the emperor had constitutional powers became irrelevant.

THE EVE OF THE SECOND WORLD WAR

The Peace Preservation Law

The Peace Preservation Law, enacted in 1925, powerfully and effectively crushed opposition. In 1928, the law was amended to include the death penalty for those found engaged in certain seditious activities. This repressive law, which violated human rights and stifled freedom of expression, together with the special political police who enforced it, formed a sinister legal means of thought control until the U.S. occupation forces ordered its revocation at the end of the war.

On March 15, 1928, some 1,568 suspected communists or sympathizers engaged in antiwar activities were arrested in one national crackdown under the Peace Preservation Law. The general secretary of the Communist Party, Watanabe Masanosuke, escaped arrest and immediately moved to rebuild the party, but the police staged another mass roundup on April 16, 1929, which destroyed the remaining party organization. Even though the party suffered a near-fatal blow, a resistance movement survived. The underground core group of the party was reconstructed repeatedly, and they continued their stubborn resistance by working with the legally sanctioned proletarian party and labor unions, social problems study groups, and proletarian cultural organizations. When Japan invaded China after the Manchurian Incident, it was the communists in the underground resistance who called for antiwar efforts.

As Kawakami Hajime of Kyoto University later revealed, believers in democracy in those days took spiritual support from the existence of an underground resistance organization—"the party," which represented a "beacon of the conscience" in dark times. Resistance began to disintegrate from about 1933, however, when imprisoned Communist Party leaders like Sano Manabu and Nabeyama Sadachika publicly renounced communism and defected from the party. The brutal enforcement of the Peace Preservation Law also took the lives of people like the eminent social scientist of the prewar years, Noro Eitarō, and the leading proletarian writer, Kobayashi Takiji. But the law's victims were not just male activists. Many women joined these battles behind the scenes and sacrificed their lives.

Tanno Setsu (1902–1987), wife of Watanabe Masanosuke, the first general secretary of the illegal Japanese Communist Party, was the head of the women's division of the party. She was arrested and sentenced to life imprisonment. In Miyagi prison, she suffered from tuberculosis and, near death, was granted a reduced sentence. Upon her release, her younger brother castigated and struck her for having brought grief to her family. Her older brother's son criticized her, saying that at school he was called the relative of a traitor. Tanno Setsu's mother could not bear the shame and attempted suicide three times.

Though Setsu endured tremendous psychological pressure, she remained deeply committed to her principles. However, other victims of the Peace Preservation Law—prosecuted for being communist sympathizers, for helping the persecuted, or for studying the social sciences—were unable to endure the harsh social oppression and committed suicide.

Women bore twice as much persecution as male advocates of ideological principles—simply because they were women. Criticism of the women resistors was not limited to the typical charge that they were "unworthy nationals" for "plotting to destroy the national polity." They also were accused of being immoral women who didn't know their place, who had sullied Japan's patriarchal family system, and who had nefariously, disrestpectfully, dared to oppose the "noble personage" of the emperor. They were treated as unforgivable social outcasts and were castigated by their home communities and relatives.

Yamashiro Tomoe, for example, was not an activist; she simply had a critical perspective no different from many others. Despite this, she was arrested and imprisoned for several years under the Peace Preservation Law. After she was released, she found that her older sister, a mother of three, had been forced to divorce because of the family's shame. Tomoe's punishment thus encompassed five people. The responsibility for the "crime" not only fell on the immediate family, but on other relatives. It was said that guilt would spread over five generations and would torment the criminal's parents, grandparents, grandchildren, and others. As a result, even those who had endured imprisonment often recanted their beliefs and knelt down to the emperor when they heard that, for example, their mother or father had committed suicide. They recognized that their actions affected not only themselves but also their innocent brothers and sisters and their children. Many resistors were unable to endure the pain of this situation.

The anguish of wives whose husbands recanted their communist principles was similarly unendurable. As Tanno Setsu recalled, "There was a man called Asano Akira, a communist and a writer. When he recanted in prison his wife, Itō Chiyoko, was unable to endure the pain. She lost her mind and was sent to Matsuzawa Hospital. She died there."*

Male intellectuals have labeled the period from 1931 to 1941 the "dark valley." But for activist women, this era was much worse than these men can imagine. In the circle of "comrades" who believed in the same principles, women often were expected to provide "services" for the male activists. The writer Kobayashi Takiji, one of the leaders of the proletarian literature movement, depicted women sacrificing themselves to the cause in this way in his novel *Tō Seikatsusha (Life as a Party Member)*.†

Unless the few remaining people who lived through this dark valley relate its history accurately, the stories of those who were victimized during this period will be forgotten. Some in the postwar generation claim that very few human rights violations occurred in Japan before the war compared with, say, the Soviet Union. They argue that, because of the "soft" nature of Japanese society, the gentle disposition of the emperor, and the relatively moderate style of government, control was not enforced with the brutality of a Hitler or Stalin.

Was this really the case? For the tens of thousands who were arrested, tortured, or killed under the Peace Preservation Law, for the more than three-thousand who were imprisoned until the end of the war, and for their family members, this period looks different. We also must not ignore the pain endured by tens of thousands of others, the victims of terror and intimidation by a government bent on control and making examples of those who resisted.

When compared to the atrocities committed at that time in Germany and the Soviet Union, life under the emperor system was indeed mild, but the treatment of nonconformists was relentless and ruthless. The thorough suppression of dissent, the witch-hunts directed against those who re-

---

*Tanno Setsu, ed. Yamashiro Tomoe and Makise Kikue (Tokyo: Keisō Shobō, 1970).

†It was published in part, heavily censored, in 1933; it was not published in full till 1945. See Donald Keene, *Dawn to the West* (New York: Henry Holt, 1984), p. 622.

jected the national polity (*kokutai*), and the unspeakable discrimination and oppression inflicted on the Korean and Chinese minorities in Japan cannot be erased from the pages of Japanese history.

When the Sky Cleared

As the Shōwa era entered its second decade in the mid-1930s, Japan won temporary relief from the economic crisis. But the respite was due, in part, to the increasing demand for war goods following the Manchurian Incident, the 1932 Shanghai Incident—when Japanese troops put down Chinese demonstrations in Shanghai and gained control of the city—and the resulting war with China. The economy enjoyed a mild recovery as Japan invaded the continent, and conditions improved for a few years during the mid-to-late 1930s.

Coffee shops and cafes catering to businessmen and students began to spring up, and about 20,000 such shops were said to exist in metropolitan Tokyo alone. Professional baseball became popular as thousands flocked to watch the games at the ballparks ("the stands," or *sutando*, as they were called). The atmosphere was like a glimmer of sunlight in the darkened sky before a storm. Jazz and musical reviews were popular, and the movie theaters, dancehalls, and bars were packed with people. Western movie classics like *The Unfinished Symphony* (1935), *The House of Mimosa* (1936), *Modern Times* (1936), and *The City of Women* (1937) were imported and shown widely.

Such activities, however, were restricted mainly to big cities like Tokyo and Osaka. Nothing so glamorous happened in the farm villages. But local plays and traveling theater groups could be seen almost anywhere, and Japan had just entered the first phase of becoming an "information society." The main actor in this important transformation was the radio. In 1932 there were only about one million radios nationwide, but eight years later, just prior to the outbreak of the Pacific War, the number had jumped to five million. Consequently, broadcasts of the government-operated radio station, NHK (Nihon Hōsō Kyōkai), could reach five million radio sets and be heard by several times that number of people—a formidable influence.

As a result of this influence, the government was able to completely mobilize the people during the Pacific War. In those days a large number of people gathered around a single radio to listen, so with one broadcast the government was able to reach and direct the people. Because of radio,

Japan's old saying, "the lord's will is the servant's command" gained universal application, even in remote farm villages.

It was during this brief period of sunlight—when people were enthralled with jazz, musical reviews, baseball, sumō, bars, dancehalls and so on—that the pivotal February 26 coup attempt took place. As a result, the February 26th Incident was somewhat removed from most people's daily lives. Rather than political events, people were interested in scandals like the Abe Sada affair. (Abe Sada became notorious overnight when she killed her lover during sex, cut off his penis, and carried it around in a bag.)

The other affair that interested people much more than the attempted coup was the Berlin Olympics. People clung to the radio for news about the games and cheered the Japanese athletes. They listened deliriously to the news about the sumō champion Futabayama's record-breaking victories. News about the February 26th Incident was censored, so people knew little more than the fact that some soldiers had attacked some politicians in Tokyo again. The general public thus did not perceive this event as serious, and its impact surfaced only slowly, later.

However, the clash with Chinese forces at the Marco Polo Bridge on the outskirts of Beijing on July 7, 1937, and the expansion of this incident into an all-out war between Japan and China affected the people instantly. A large number of soldiers were called to arms and were sent to the battlefront by flag-waving villagers and townspeople. Slogans like "national emergency," "life of austerity," and "untiring perseverance" suddenly were everywhere. At that time Japanese people paid little attention to Germany's declaration of its plan to rearm, the conclusion of the Japanese-German Anti-Comintern Pact, the Italian invasion of Ethiopia, or the outbreak of the Spanish Civil War. No one imagined that these events would have a decisive impact on Japan several years later.

The Spanish Civil War and Japan's International Consciousness

When the Spanish Civil War broke out in 1936, international volunteer brigades were organized to support the popular front government of Spain. The organizers warned that if the Spanish government fell to the fascist forces of Generalissimo Franco, who had Hitler's backing, fascism would soon control Europe and a major war would follow. Tens of thousands of volunteers joined the fight, from the European nations, the United States, China, the Soviet Union, and even from Germany, where the volunteers had to evade the authorities to get to the battlefields of Spain. At the time, France also was headed by a popular front government, so a large number of French fighters, from anarchists to liberals, joined the volunteer brigades. From New York, the Abraham Lincoln Brigade crossed the sea to fight the fascists. All the volunteers were armed with idealistic concepts like international solidarity.

But in Japan neither the labor unions nor the intellectuals displayed any reaction to these developments. A few Japanese intellectuals and writers were aware of the struggle and the international outcry and some magazine stories were written, but almost no one considered joining the volunteers in the battlefield. A few Japanese did join up, one of whom enlisted in the group from the United States. Jack Shirai, who was then working in New York, joined the Abraham Lincoln Brigade and died in battle near Madrid. Jack Shirai's grave is now honored among those of the heroes of the international volunteer army.

The final stage of the Spanish Civil War ended with betrayal by the Soviet Union. Stalin suddenly ended Soviet military assistance and ordered the Soviet brigade to withdraw from the international volunteer army, in part because of his plan to make a deal with Nazi Germany. The governments of England and France also hoped to bargain with Hitler and abandoned Spain. Without this outside support, the Spanish popular front government was forced to surrender to Franco. At this time, intellectuals in France, England, the United States, and Germany angrily criticized Stalinism as an inhuman ideology wearing the mask of Marxism; they saw this betrayal as either a callous rejection of world revolution or a confirmation that the regime was totalitarian.

Many Japanese intellectuals, however, were ignorant of these issues. They glorified Stalin and held the Soviet Union up as their ideal until long after the war, when Khrushchev publicly criticized Stalin. But they were behind the times of international affairs by at least twenty years. This time lag sprang from their ignorance of the world and their refusal to consider the problems confronting Japan in the context of global developments and world history. Developments in Japan must not be analyzed simply in terms of Japan itself; Japanese history must be reexamined from a global perspective.

The same principle applies to the relationship between Japan and China. It should have been possible to find a local solution to the clash between Japanese and Chinese forces at the Marco Polo Bridge on the outskirts of Beijing on July 7, 1937. Why did this skirmish spread throughout China? Why did it trigger the Pacific War? We cannot answer these questions unless we consider the important events in China in December, 1936—the Xian Incident.

The Xian Incident and Japan's Historical Blindness

The Xian Incident began on December 12, 1936, when Jiang Jieshi (Chiang Kai-shek), president of the Republic of China, flew to the city of Xian to oversee his planned offensive against the Chinese Communist Party's liberated zone. But upon arrival, Jiang was arrested and detained by his own troops under the command of Zhang Xueliang, a powerful Manchurian warlord and the son of Zhang Zuolin (who had been assassinated by the Japanese in 1928). Zhang's troops had no desire to fight a civil war against the communists while Japanese forces occupied their homeland. Jiang Jieshi was about to be executed when Zhou Enlai flew in from the communist-held zone and prevented his death. Zhou instead persuaded Jiang that the Chinese people were facing a crisis, that they should end the internal conflict and join to fight Japanese imperialism. This agreement initiated the united front of the nationalists and the communists, a partnership that soon led to all-out war with Japan.

At first, Jiang Jieshi was obsessed with hatred for Zhang Xueliang who, he felt, had unjustly arrested and detained him in Xian. After returning to Shanghai, he even considered scrapping the agreement with Zhou Enlai, even though Zhou had saved his life. But when word of the agreement between the communist and nationalist forces spread throughout China, wild street demonstrations celebrating the alliance and attacking Japanese aggression broke out among students and workers in Shanghai, Beijing, Nanjing, Xian—throughout the land. Jiang Jieshi realized that he could not go against this kind of popular, emotional sentiment. Chinese public opinion was at a boiling point, and the result was the successful formation of the Anti-Japanese People's United Front. This movement crushed Japanese imperialism and determined the future course of history in Asia.

Some well-informed Japanese were aware of the significance of these developments. But Japanese journalists were extremely insensitive to Chinese matters and paid little notice—and, of course, the militarists paid no attention either. If the militarists had fully appreciated the political significance of the Xian Incident, they might have hesitated to instigate the kind of military provocation that they staged the following year at the Marco Polo Bridge outside Beijing, for when the communists and nationalists joined together, Chinese military power essentially doubled. Once the

Anti-Japanese People's United Front had been organized throughout China, a war between Japan and China could only be a war of attrition for Japan, fought in a quagmire against a united population of 600 million. The inability to perceive this situation in China after the Xian Incident was ultimately the most important reason for Japan's defeat in the Second World War, even more important than the war with the United States

Among the military men, Ishiwara Kanji (one of the architects of the Manchurian Incident) was somewhat more aware that engaging the entire Chinese population would be disastrous. Ishiwara's war plan was designed to focus instead on the behemoth to the north—Japan's old enemy, Russia. Ishiwara understood that a protracted war in China would deplete Japan's power and ultimately leave Japan powerless against other foes. Ishiwara felt that the "final war" would be fought with the United States in the middle of the Pacific Ocean. Before that, however, the Soviet Union had to be crushed. Total war with China was out of the question, for it would result only in a long, draining, and indecisive struggle.

But Ishiwara's plan was never adopted. He was removed from key military positions and placed in semi-internment by mainstream army officers, including General Tōjō Hideki (later Japan's prime minister). From their narrow perspective, these officers could not grasp the important changes that had moved China from civil war to a vigorous united front.

The international situation was changing fast. Ignoring important developments such as the increasing emergence of the Soviet Union, Japan adhered to its old policy of aggression on the continent. There was talk of attacking north, talk of attacking south. With its leaders focusing shortsightedly on the use of force for immediate ends, it was inevitable that Japan would dig its own grave. Those leaders—including the emperor—who failed to comprehend the international realities bear a heavy responsibility to the people of Japan.

In September 1940 the Tripartite Alliance was concluded by Japan, Germany, and Italy. The following month, the cabinet headed by Prince Konoe Fumimaro (who was prime minister) disbanded all political parties and organized the Imperial Rule Assistance Association, which aimed to foster "loyalty in assisting imperial rule." Intended as a mass movement, the association ultimately failed as a political organization. But by this time neither of the two major parties, the Seiyūkai and the Minseitō, was capable of restraining the military and consolidating political power. The labor unions also lost their political influence. They submitted to bureaucratic control and were compelled to restructure themselves into the Great Japanese Industrial Patriotic Association.

A small group of imperial advisors sought to avoid a confrontation with the United States, but the army decided to attack south. Ignoring warnings from the United States, it sent troops into northern Vietnam and then occupied the entire country. Unable to ignore these moves, the United States applied economic sanctions against Japan and made the Japanese withdrawal from China and Vietnam the condition for their removal. These sanctions, including a crippling embargo on oil and steel supplies, presented Japan with an ultimatum. The emperor, shaken by this development, vacillated but ultimately consented to the decision by the government led by General Tōjō Hideki to go to war against the United States.

To Soviet Sakhalin in the Snow

Another mysterious episode can help us rethink the course of history: the defection of Sugimoto Ryōkichi and Okada Yoshiko. On January 3, 1938, Sugimoto Ryōkichi, a modern playwright, and Okada Yoshiko, a popular and beautiful actress, boldly crossed the border on the northern island of Sakhalin and entered the Soviet Union. Then they disappeared.

Fifty years later, under Soviet *perestroika*, the truth about the two defectors was made public by Japanese researchers. After crossing into Soviet territory, they met tragedy. Sugimoto, at that time a Japanese Communist Party member who was being pursued by the special political police, believed that the Soviet Union was a liberated country. But upon arrival he was arrested, imprisoned as a spy, and tortured. Then, as Okada Yoshiko has written in recent newspaper accounts, he was shot in prison the following year. Okada Yoshiko also endured terrible hardships in a Soviet internment camp, but she was later released and allowed to work in the theater as an actress.

Why did the Soviet Union execute a man who had absolute faith in it as the true friend of the oppressed, a comrade who sought refuge in "the homeland of revolution and freedom"? Half a year before Okada and Sugimoto crossed the border in May 1937, Stalin accused Marshal Tukhachevsky and other top army leaders of plotting to overthrow the Soviet government by conspiring with German fascists. He tried and executed them in June. The Tukhachevsky affair plunged the Soviet Union into the Great Purge. When the two defectors arrived, Stalin was conducting wholesale arrests of everyone among his former revolutionary comrades and their associates who was in any way critical of him. Many people were either exiled in Siberia or shot. It now appears that Sugimoto was a sacri-

ficial lamb in Stalin's plot to eliminate Meyerhold, the leading Soviet theater director. Stalin wanted to eliminate all cultural and intellectual figures
who did not strictly adhere to socialist realism. Because Meyerhold had
criticized this artistic style, Stalin wanted to purge him and everyone
under his influence in the theatrical world. Sugimoto evidently was suspected of belonging to Meyerhold's circle. Sugimoto Ryōkichi and Okada
Yoshiko leaped into this situation with no idea of what was happening in
the Soviet Union.

By the time of the defections, the Japanese state had a complete monopoly on all information, and news from the outside rarely reached the
people. As a result, the Japanese public had no knowledge of conditions in
the Soviet Union under Stalin. The execution of Marshal Tukhachevsky
was reported in the press, but not the incarceration of millions of political
prisoners in the new Siberian gulag. (But even if such reports had reached
Japan, communist idealists probably would have dismissed them as lies
perpetrated by the bourgeois press.)

As this painful incident illustrates, most world news was not available
to the Japanese people. The few people who had access to information,
such as journalists covering the war, were restricted from communicating
what they knew.

Some people did desperately try to convey the truth. These included
Kiryū Yūyū, the editor-in-chief of the *Shinano Daily News;* Kikutake Rokko,
the editor-in-chief of the *Fukuoka Daily News;* Masaki Hiroshi, a lawyer
who carried on his struggle against the authorities by publishing the journal *Chikaki Yori (From Nearby);* and Yanaihara Tadao, a Christian who continued his stubborn resistance by publishing the small personal journal
Kashin (Blessed Faith), yet these and other such people were few.

Most people read the major newspapers, which were told what to report and which uncritically obeyed. The only access to international news
was NHK radio, which was also under the government's thumb. The news
reported by these media was strictly censored by the army and navy information bureaus or by the Home Ministry and cabinet information
bureaus.

Access to world information is one decisive difference between Japan
then and now. Today, it is impossible for a government to exercise such
complete control over the information its people receive. Unless we realize
how limited their knowledge was, it is easy to be critical of the Japanese
people of that time. It is too harsh to condemn the people, who were deprived of information by the government and the military. They did not

have access to knowledge that would have enabled them to make better judgments.

While part of the world was embracing fascism, the Japanese lacked the information needed to stand their ground and say "wait." It was the responsibility of the intellectuals to help people grasp the situation; compared with most people, the intellectuals were in a far better position to obtain information from abroad. Had they even tried to discuss the true international situation, however, they would have come under state surveillance and their lives would have been threatened by the Peace Preservation Law. But the fact that intellectuals did not dare take that risk is a stigma that still clings.

The dominant ideologies that suppressed information were the so-called "national polity" (*kokutai*) and the emperor system (*tennōsei*). The ideology of national polity enveloped the entire Japanese nation. It had an incredible presence. It is difficult to imagine the oppressive atmosphere that the people suffered under the canopy of national polity and the immutable emperor system. There was complete social consensus that those who violated these ideologies should be eliminated or that they inevitably would be eliminated.

Most importantly, the Peace Preservation Law made anyone who criticized or advocated changing the Japanese national polity a target of punishment, and in 1928 the death penalty was added to bolster the threat. It was under this kind of intellectual climate that the ordinary people of Japan submitted to the authorities, and we should keep this idea in mind when we consider the problems of wartime Japan.

Luxury Is the Enemy

As Japan and China moved toward total war, the Japanese government devised numerous policies and regulatory laws to cope with the increasing shortages of goods. In April 1938 the National Mobilization Law was enacted, enabling the government to impose controls over human and economic resources. The law banned the free transaction of some commercial goods in the open market, and prices of essential commodities came under the jurisdiction of government bureaucrats. The use of natural gas was restricted, and rice, the staple food, and clothing were strictly rationed by household.

When the Second World War broke out in Europe in September 1939, regulatory controls in Japan became increasingly stringent. The following year, the decree banning luxury goods was issued. Next, men with long hair were told to cut it short and eventually were ordered to have crew cuts, like soldiers. For women, permanents were outlawed. Women were also forbidden from wearing long-sleeved kimonos, and ladies of the Patriotic Women's Association would cut off the offending sleeves if any woman wore them in public. Women also were forced to wear ugly clothes, like the ubiquitous baggy trousers called *monpe*. The public was prohibited from wearing Western-style suits, and even dancehalls and bars were banned as "enemy customs." The war thus was not only the exchange of gunfire on distant battlefields; it was felt in every aspect of Japanese daily life.

The short economic spring was soon blown away, and people once more faced scarcity and deprivation. This burden fell mainly on women, who were defending the homefront in the households and factories. They had to take care of the elderly, send the older children to school, and safeguard the small children in the family. It was a time of food shortages, and mothers were expected to reduce their own consumption so that the children and men had a little more food.

In the fall of 1943, I graduated from the Second Higher School in Sendai and went to college in Tokyo. I rented a room from a railroad worker's kind family in Ichikawa, just outside Tokyo in Chiba prefecture, and commuted to college in the Hongō section of Tokyo. There were four children in the family, but the eldest daughter was serving in the women's volunteer corps, so five family members were in the household at that time.

The mother of the household was in her early forties. Their rice ration was very meager. After the mother had served a bowl of rice to each of her children, nothing was left in the pot. I was a boarder, so she served me my share of the rice ration, which was about the same amount that the children received. Though there was nothing left for the mother, she put a few grains of rice in her bowl to make it look as though she had eaten. The children noticed this and said, "Mother, you've got to eat," and tried to give her some of their rice. But she replied, "No, there's more in the kitchen. I'm going to eat after all of you have finished." But she hardly ate anything. Instead, she sometimes would drink hot water in the kitchen to assuage her hunger. Although she was pale and emaciated, she made certain that her husband had enough to eat because, she said, he had to work hard at the railroad. I clearly saw the effects of the patriarchal family system in this family suffering from material scarcity, and I still cannot erase the image of that mother from my mind.

In those days, there were many women trying desperately to ensure the health of their children by cutting back on their own food. As members of their neighborhood associations, one responsibility of women was to send off conscripted soldiers by cheering, waving the national flag, and praying for victory. But whenever they had spare time, they went to the farm villages with sacks on their backs in search of sweet potatoes and other edible goods. Sometimes they brought along a kimono, perhaps the kimono and sash they had brought with them when they were married, to exchange for potatoes and pumpkins to keep their families from starving.

These ordinary women who struggled so desperately during the war should not be condemned as its supporters. They had no choice but to carry on and support the war effort. The scarcity continued for four to five years, and women also suffered air raids, bombings, compulsory evacuation, and the dispersal of their families. The war for these women involved enduring and rising above these hardships.

Paradoxically, Japan's war—like all modern wars—advanced the cause of women's liberation. Because the men had left for the battlefield, women on the homefront had to enter the workplace to do what had been men's work. But this loosening of gender-based occupational specialization was accomplished through indescribable sacrifices by women. Women's postwar advancement was largely the result of their role during the war.

THE PACIFIC WAR AND THE EXPERIENCE OF DEFEAT

A Complex and Strange World

When Prime Minister Hiranuma Kiichirō resigned along with his cabinet in August 1939 (following the announcement of the Nazi-Soviet pact, which stunned Japan's militarist government), he remarked that the situation in Europe was "complex and strange." Japan's other political leaders were similarly puzzled by the global situation and failed to perceive the direction in which the world was moving. As a result, they staked the fate of Japan on Hitler, who then seemed to be headed for victory. With hindsight, though, it is clear that Japan's leaders had once again pushed the nation against the general current of history.

Increasingly, the Japanese were groping along the edge of a cliff. Nazi

Germany soon occupied Paris and nearly conquered all of Europe. The German army also advanced to a point seven kilometers from Moscow and occupied all of the Balkan peninsula; North Africa eventually was under the control of the combined forces of Germany and Italy. The Allied forces were driven out of the European continent, and only England, entrenched on its little island, was still barely holding out.

Though the Japanese army, seeing these developments, decided that events were moving in favor of Germany, the navy went along only reluctantly. The mainstream naval officers were reluctant to engage England and the United States in a war, but finally concluded that England was likely to surrender because Germany was gaining so many victories. If England surrendered, the communist government of Russia would collapse too. Unless they made a deal with Germany at that moment, Japan's military and political leaders thought, Japan would not share the spoils after the Axis victory. This reasoning seemed sound in 1940, but the course of world events was very precarious. History does not necessarily unfold as planned or envisioned by leaders.

Japan's leaders were significantly out of step with world historical currents in other areas, as well. China was not, as Japanese leaders believed, fragmented into separate regions by warlords and therefore powerless. It had already been unified both as the nationalist Republic of China and under the communists in their liberated zones. It was rapidly getting back on its feet. Moreover, the Chinese people were aroused by a strong nationalist fervor. Misunderstanding of this situation led Japan to make several brazen mistakes. After the First World War, Japan took over the German holdings in Shandong Province in China, and Chinese resentment of this occupation was further enflamed by the assassination of Zhang Zuolin, the Manchurian Incident and the resultant colonization of northeastern China, and the brutal attack on the Chinese capital of Nanjing in December 1937.

In 1928 the Kellogg-Briand international peace pact, which prohibited war as a solution to international disputes, was concluded in Paris. When Japanese leaders were tried for war crimes at the Far East International Military Tribunal after World War II, some criticized the trial as a one-sided, unfair show trial conducted arbitrarily by the victors. But Japan had ratified the 1928 international peace pact in the name of the emperor and thus invited condemnation as an aggressor nation by resorting to force to resolve international disputes and by occupying Manchuria without recourse to diplomatic negotiations. It is regrettable that the Japanese leaders ignored the pact's principles: they regarded such treaties as pieces of paper to be used temporarily and, under certain circumstances, simply discarded. Twenty years later they were to learn their lesson in the Tokyo war crimes trials of 1948.

The War Between Japan and the United States

Japanese forces were spectacularly successful during the first seven months of the Pacific War, occupying New Guinea near Australia to the south and the Aleutian islands to the north. To the west, they moved into Burma and pushed to the borders of India. Japanese forces expanded into a vast region: nearly one-seventh of the earth's surface.

But then the course of events reversed, and Japan went on the defensive. In the south in early 1943 it suffered a major defeat at Guadalcanal, and in the north the imperial forces were totally annihilated by the U.S. offensive in Attu. In the center, American forces broke the Japanese line of defense at Truk and rapidly turned the tide. Then, in the summer of 1944, seven aircraft carriers, along with vital squadrons of aircraft, were sunk in the naval battle off the Mariana islands. In July, following this decisive naval defeat, the Japanese troops defending Saipan were annihilated. At the same time came news of defeat in Burma. The time had come for Japan to end the war.

Because of these defeats in 1944, Prime Minister Tōjō Hideki was forced to resign, presenting the Japanese people with an excellent opportunity to achieve peace. If the leaders had moved to end the war then by having the emperor make his "sacred decision" (the emperor's announcement on August 15, 1945, that Japan would agree to the conditions of the Potsdam declaration), 1.5 million Japanese lives would have been saved, as well as the lives of twice that many Asians.

Following the defeat at the Mariana islands and the fall of Saipan, the war plan conference of the Imperial Headquarters did conclude that Japan had no chance of winning the war. They stated that "we can no longer conduct the war with any hope of success" and that "there was unanimous agreement that henceforth Japan will only undergo gradual deterioration, so plans should be devised to end the war quickly."*

The leaders of the Imperial Headquarters, however, dragged out the war for thirteen more months after arriving at this conclusion. The reasons

*Daihonei Kimitsu Sensō Nisshi (Secret War Journal of the Imperial Headquarters), entry for July 1, 1944. The journal is in the archives of the Defense Agency Research Center.

why they did not have the "noble decision" proclaimed sooner have yet to be fully clarified and should be examined in greater depth.

From the fall of Saipan in July 1944, when the military leaders concluded that there was no chance of victory, to the end of the war in 1945, 1.5 million Japanese died. In the first half of 1945 alone 1 million people died. Close to 300,000 residents of Hiroshima and Nagasaki, 200,000 Okinawans, 200,000 retreating forces in Burma, and 200,000 in Manchuria, including Japanese civilians, were killed. The largest number died in the Philippines: 400,000, including those who perished in jungle warfare. And 200,000 people died in air raids on Japan itself. Many times more people were killed in Southeast Asia, the Pacific islands, and China, and during this period the United States lost over 50,000 young soldiers.

The war ended when the emperor finally delivered his "noble decision" on August 15, 1945. To absolve the emperor of all responsibility for the war because of his decision to end it is to ignore the facts presented in the preceding pages. The emperor's close advisers and scholars naturally wanted to defend him, but the Shōwa emperor must have felt personally responsible for his poor leadership during the war.

The Emperor's Soliloquy

Those who have examined the notes of the emperor's close advisers have conjectured that the emperor felt that Japan should first "thoroughly beat the enemy before negotiating" or should negotiate only after Japan had "seized an opportunity for victory." But the recently uncovered personal recollections of Emperor Hirohito (*Tennō Dokuhaku Roku*) makes his thoughts on these matters very clear. (In late 1990, a two-volume manuscript of notes prepared by Terasaki Hidenari, an advisor to the emperor just after the war, was made public by Terasaki's daughter, Mariko. The material consists of the emperor's testimony on the war, to be presented if he were called upon to testify at the Tokyo war crimes trials. This manuscript was published in the December 1990 issue of the journal *Bungei Shunjū*. The entire document is perhaps the most important postwar historical discovery, a first-rate historical document, and has been published as a book under the title *The Soliloquy of the Shōwa Emperor: The Record of Imperial Court Attendant Terasaki Hidenari* [Tokyo: Bungei Shunjū, 1991]. The following excerpts of the emperor's comments, as well as the accompanying notes by the editor, Bantō Kazutoshi, are from this book.)

Even after Japan's defeat in the battle of Okinawa, the emperor recalled,

In Okinawa, it was clear that there was no hope for victory in a naval battle. The only hope was to strike against the forces in Yunnan in conjunction with the Burma campaign. This should have been a heavy blow against England and America. I suggested this to Umezu [General Umezu Yoshijirō, Army Chief of Staff], but he opposed the plan saying we would not be able to provide the troops with the necessary supplies and reinforcements. When I spoke to Prince Kaya, who was then president of the Army College, he replied that it might succeed temporarily. He said he would study the situation, but nothing ever came of it.

Bantō Kazutoshi, who annotated the imperial comments and wrote an analysis of the document, paid special attention to these few lines. Commenting on the proposal to launch a campaign in Yunnan, he wrote, "this is a dramatic example of the emperor's 'commander-in-chief'-style personality." Many other entries in the document show the emperor speaking on important matters of national policy and military strategy and actively giving his advice or instruction. This document has thus been highly inconvenient for pro-imperial scholars, who have endeavored to clear the emperor of all responsiblity. Itō Takashi, a conservative professor at Tokyo University, was the first Japanese scholar to be shown this record of the emperor's personal remarks. He spoke honestly when he said, "to tell the truth, this is a highly disturbing document."

The emperor continued:

Since it was decided that there was no longer any hope of success for the Yunnan war plan, I decided that there was no other way out but to call for a negotiated peace. . . . The imperial conference of June, which was held prior to the interim Diet meeting, was truly a strange affair. At that time, Umezu was on a trip to Manchuria so the army Vice Chief of Staff [Kawabe Torajirō] was present in his place as Chief of Staff. According to the government's report taking all information into account, it was impossible to continue with the war. Despite this conclusion, Navy Chief of Staff Toyoda [Fukutake] and the Army Vice Chief of Staff insisted that the war be continued because there was no question that victory could be achieved. This argument, that there was no question that we would win the war, completely contradicted the government's report, but ultimately the conference decided to continue the war.

Here the emperor states that he had decided on a negotiated peace, but then tries to distance himself from this position, as if he were merely a media commentator. Referring to Hiranuma Kiichirō, a staunch nationalist and an imperial advisor, the emperor further remarks, "Hiranuma's attitude at this meeting was crafty. . . . He said those who oppose the war should be punished forcefully." Also,

> Toyoda Fukutake, who insisted on continuing the war, is not a person with whom one can agree. He just talks tough. Because of this, we have disagreements between the army and navy. He failed as commander of the Mariana campaign. I had once told Yonai [Yonai Mitsumasa, naval minister and former prime minister] that it is a mistake to appoint a person whose record as naval commander is poor to the post of navy chief of staff.
> Yonai said he must insist on doing so.

Though the emperor complains about those who wanted to continue the war, he did not take any action to save the nation. During this time, Tokyo and all the major cities were being laid waste by the air raids. Economic production had collapsed, and it was then hastily decided to send Konoe Fumimaro to Moscow as a special envoy in July 1945.

At the Yalta Conference of February 1945, Stalin secretly had agreed to join the war against Japan, so naturally he did not respond to Japan's request for mediation. Hitler was already dead (April 30th), Germany had surrendered unconditionally (May 7th), and it was obvious that Japan would be defeated soon. Those who believed that the Soviet Union would cooperate with Japan and act on its behalf were abysmally ignorant of foreign affairs.

Japanese policy toward the Soviet Union at this final desperate stage can be illuminated further by quoting the emperor in the *Soliloquy*. This account was recorded during March and April of 1946, so the emperor was recalling events that had transpired about eight months earlier.

> I . . . summoned the members of the Supreme Leadership Conference and told them to quickly prepare for peace negotiations. I don't recall if I told them to do this by Soviet mediation. At this point, Suzuki [Prime Minister Suzuki Kantarō] and others suggested that we should check out the Soviets' intentions. I told them that was a good idea. Because of the current circumstances, we had to arrange for a swift resolution of the situation. . . . But it was agreed that the Soviet Union was not a country with sincere intentions, so we wanted to first feel them out. It was decided to proceed with talks between Hirota [Hirota Kōki, former foreign minister and prime minister] and Yakov Malik [Soviet ambassador to Japan]. If the Soviet Union would agree to ship oil to

Japan, Hirota was to tell Malik that Japan would be willing to transfer south Sakhalin or even Manchuria to the Soviet Union. But even in early July there was no response from the Soviet Union.

From our point of view, matters had to be settled before the Potsdam conference convened. Further delay would be troublesome for us. I conferred with Suzuki and we decided to terminate the discussions between Hirota and Malik, and negotiate directly with the Soviet government. We considered who might be the most suitable person to send to Moscow, and decided that Konoe would be the best. But others felt that Konoe would be reluctant to undertake this assignment. So I decided to speak to Konoe myself.

I believe it was early in July. I summoned Konoe and asked him to undertake the assignment even though it would be difficult. Konoe agreed to undertake the mission, saying that he would do his best to accomplish it.

Suzuki was delighted to hear this and informed the Soviet authorities that we wished to send Konoe, but also requested their assistance in initiating negotiations for peace with England and America. Thereupon, the Soviet authorities replied that they would respond after their officials had returned from the Potsdam conference. These matters are noted in detail in the notes of Chief Cabinet Secretary Sakomizu Hisatsune [*Kōfukuji no Shinsō (The True Account of the Surrender)*] so I will not discuss them here. Stalin did not respond even after he returned from Potsdam. Unfortunately, soon after that the Soviet Union declared war on Japan. Faced with this we felt that there was no alternative but unconditional surrender.

The air raids increased in intensity daily. The atomic bomb made its appearance on August 6th. The people were in desperate straits. The Soviet Union commenced fighting in Manchuria. Thus we were forced into a situation in which we had to accept the terms of the Potsdam Declaration.

This account indicates that the Japanese leaders were not simply thinking of turning over the four northern islands (the Kuriles). The emperor, his close advisers, the prime minister, and others were willing to give southern Sakhalin and Manchuria to the Soviet Union in exchange for supplying Japan with oil. There is no indication that they understood why the Soviet Union did not respond to the Japanese request. These passages make it clear that the "noble decision" to surrender was made after the emperor realized that "there was no alternative but unconditional surrender" following the atomic bombings and the entry of the Soviet Union into the war.

War Weariness and the Great Air Raids

In 1945, as air raids by U.S. planes flying out of Saipan grew increasingly intense, food shortages and inflation became more serious and the economic life of the people worsened very rapidly. The country had been on the verge of a standstill. Then the massive air raids on Japan made its people realize that all was lost. Especially damaging was the horrendous blanket bombing by B-29s, starting in March 1945. The first large-scale raid was conducted against Tokyo at midnight on March 9th. In just one night 98,000 Tokyo citizens were killed, well over 200,000 houses burned down, and 1 million people were burned out of their homes.

There is a limit to what people can endure. Even though no one spoke openly, this mass killing—unique in history—spread war weariness among the people. If anyone had spoken out (as some did, in anonymous graffiti, for example), they would have been attacked as "unpatriotic," denied their food rations, or arrested by the special political police or the military police, and their entire family would have suffered. There was no recourse but to suffer in silence.

There was another factor: people had been so thoroughly brainwashed by the imperial educational system that they simply endured the wartime suffering. They had been taught that Japan was led by a living god, the emperor, and blessed by the sun goddess, Amaterasu Ōmikami, and so could not lose the war. Surrender was out of the question. Thus, even though the difficulties of daily life fanned antiwar sentiment, people did not believe that Japan would surrender. Today this attitude seems irrational, but then such an atmosphere was prevalent. People thus were unable to go beyond harboring antiwar sentiments to actually protest against the war.

Air raids became almost a daily occurence in different cities throughout Japan. In the May 25, 1945, air raid on Tokyo the imperial palace grounds—the symbol of Japan, the land of the gods—burned down. All of the imperial family's houses were destroyed, and many firefighters died in their effort to save the imperial family members. It is said that fear drove the empress into a frenzy.

The following month, Okinawa fell. Faced with these developments, the emperor began to seriously consider ending the war. Former Prime Minister Konoe Fumimaro had submitted a memorandum to the emperor in February of that year stating that the only option was to negotiate an end to the war. But the emperor did not adopt his proposal. He delayed, saying that Japan should continue until the enemy had been thoroughly beaten. He reasoned that because the military was preparing a new strategy, he should wait until the "opportunity for victory" had been seized.

During this period, over 10 million people saw their cities and homes burned in the air raids. The summer of 1945 was a horrendous time, essential to any discussion of Shōwa history. The people—mainly women, children, and the elderly—who lived in farm villages or who had been evacuted there did not suffer directly from these raids and were fortunate. But they, too, were plagued by fears and worries. Their fathers, husbands, or sons were probably working in factories that were bombing targets. Some were on the battlefields, some had been conscripted and were laboring in some unknown place, perhaps a foreign land. A telegram informing them of the death of their loved one could arrive at any moment. They may have sat before Shintō or Buddhist altars every morning to pray, but nothing could calm their worry.

An old man who listened to the emperor issuing the command to surrender on the radio on August 15, 1945, cried out in despair. "This is stupid. If the war could be stopped by the emperor simply raising his hands and surrendering, why didn't he end the war sooner for us? Your Majesty, because of this my sons have all died in vain, a dog's death." His two sons, who had been conscripted as students to work in factories just before the end of the war, had died in air raids.*

In addition, Chinese, Koreans, Taiwanese, and other Asians had their homelands and nationalities taken away, were conscripted into the army, and never returned home. Asian victims totaled ten to fifteen times the number of Japanese victims whose homes burned or who lost their lives. We must not forget the bitterness of countless victims in China, Korea, Southeast Asia, Burma, India, and the South Pacific islands. Even forty-five years after the end of the war, Japan had not formally apologized to these people or compensated them. Can such a nation be said to have any moral principles?

Unconditional Surrender

For Japan to surrender unconditionally and be occupied by foreign military forces was an unprecedented, stupefying event. On September 8, 1945, the Supreme Commander of the Allied Powers, General Douglas MacArthur, advanced with a train of jeeps toward Tokyo and the emperor's

---

*'*Nagoya Daikūshū*' ('*The Great Nagoya Air Raid*'), ed. Mainichi Shinbun (Tokyo: Mainichi Shinbunsha,1971).

residence. Journalists from all over the world watched, probably curious about how Japan, the land of the *kamikaze* pilots and *harakiri* samurai, would react to this humiliation. They naturally assumed that there would be guerrilla resistance or a general panic.

As it turned out, the people of Japan remained completely calm. Not a single shot was fired against the occupation forces. The foreign observors were surprised once again at how the emperor's command was obeyed so completely. The expectation that the army would stage a coup if the emperor ordered a surrender was mistaken.

On September 9, the day after he hoisted the American flag in Tokyo, General MacArthur issued a proclamation on how the occupation would be conducted. He announced that martial law would not be imposed; instead, the occupying forces would rule indirectly by having their directives carried out by the Japanese government. This policy was designed to make the most effective use of the governing authority of the emperor and the Japanese bureaucratic system.

MacArthur established the General Headquarters of the Allied Powers (hereafter referred to as GHQ, as it is commonly known in Japan) in the Dai-ichi building, across from the imperial palace, and brought the Japanese government under the authority of the Central Liaison Office for concluding the war. He issued a series of rapid-fire orders and proceeded to abolish the military system, disarm the fighting forces, and confiscate and destroy weapons and war production plants. There were still enormous quantities of Japanese warships, airplanes, vehicles, artillery, ammunition, and other equipment, which MacArthur ordered to be converted into scrap iron, burned, or dumped into the sea. The military, which had bandied slogans like "A Hundred Million Special Attack Troops," "Decisive Battle on Japanese Soil," and "Indestructable Land of the Gods," surrendered without firing a single shot at the forces they had been calling "American and English devils." These developments flabbergasted the Japanese people. Were these leaders simply paper tigers who talked big? Were they the docile lambs of the emperor, the commander-in-chief? The depth of their disappointment was one reason why the Japanese people's sense of values collapsed.

As if to counter this sentiment, Prince Higashikuni, the prime minister who was responsible for the Nanjing massacre, called on all 100 milllion Japanese people to repent and ask the emperor's forgiveness for the sin of having caused Japan's defeat. The major communications media went along with this line of thinking. I do not know of any other instance in which history was so shackled and distorted—and I have never been so disappointed as when the Japanese people accepted it.

The acceptance of the Potsdam Declaration and the end of the fighting did not immediately improve living conditions. On the contrary, because of the food shortage immediately after the defeat, some estimated that 10 million people were likely to starve to death. At that time, a steady stream of expatriate Japanese and demobilized troops were returning from the continent, and no food was available for them. A total of 7 million hungry people returned to Japan, where residents had hardly any food to eat themselves. The harvest of 1945 was one of the worst rice and wheat crop failures in history. Because of insufficient fertilizer, a shortage of workers, and the farmers' lack of motivation to produce, only a small amount of rice and wheat was harvested. With the veterans returning, famine ensued.

Although not as many people starved to death as had been feared, the death toll was high. On a few occasions I saw trucks in metropolitan Tokyo headed for the crematory, piled high with those who had starved to death. And many people were on the verge of starvation in Tokyo neighborhoods like Shinbashi and Ikebukuro and in the subway tunnels of Ueno. About 2,000 people were sleeping in railroad stations and subways, in the midst of excrement and trash; their clothes were filthy and they smelled terrible. Among the large number of people sleeping in Ueno Park were many who froze overnight and never woke up. Sanitation department workers then transported these bodies to be burned.

A large number of people collapsed and died from malnutrition. Many—especially mothers and babies—were so weak that they died suddenly if they caught a cold. Many young men caught tuberculosis, coughed up a large amount of blood, and died. I had part of my right lung removed because of tuberculosis. In those days people almost felt out of place if they *didn't* have tuberculosis. People caught the disease because of extreme malnutrition, so death from tuberculosis was another form of death from starvation. If the people who died of sickness and of general physical deterioration are classified among those who died of starvation, the death toll comes to several hundred thousand.

For two or three years there were also many vagrants, homeless children, prostitutes, and wounded veterans in Tokyo, Osaka, and other cities. The writer Nozaka Akiyuki was one such homeless child, and one of his short novels, *Hotaru no Haka (A Grave of Fireflies)*, is about his experience with his younger sister, who died of starvation.

During this period, China was going through a revolution. A revolutionary storm of fervor and idealism to liberate the people—not unlike the developments in Eastern Europe in 1989—was sweeping across the entire country. This storm spread into the neighboring countries and gave rise to new, independent people's states, one after another.

In Japan, the GHQ led by the U.S. occupation forces issued directive after directive to impose reforms, which, if left to the Japanese government, would never have been implemented. The first of these reforms was the liberation of women. This step was truly impressive, and without this measure Japan would not have been able to rise from its ruins. Thus in Japan, too, the revolutionary storm of Asia, in a different form, developed very swiftly.

The Peace Preservation Law was eliminated, and the GHQ ordered the release of over three-thousand political prisoners. The current secretary general of the Communist Party, Miyamoto Kenji, was among those who were released. Freedom of speech was restored. Other reforms followed, including land reform, the dissolution of the *zaibatsu* (financial-industrial conglomerates), and promotion of the organization of labor unions. Educational reforms, the adoption of a new constitution, and other reforms were introduced soon after.

The Japanese government, still led by men dedicated to preserving the national polity, had no desire to adopt these democratic reforms and, indeed, tried to sabotage them. The cabinet headed by Prince Higashikuni resigned when GHQ overruled their resistance, and then the process of democratization proceeded under pressure from the military occupation authorities. To achieve this goal, a strict system of censorship was imposed. In the early stage of the occupation, GHQ carried out thorough democratic reforms in all areas in order to ensure that Japan could not be reborn as a major military power. As a result, Japan was relieved of the burden of heavy military expenditures, and the Japanese economy was able to develop as a powerful force, eventually surpassing the United States. The American reformers, undoubtedly, did not imagine such a situation arising.

The introduction of these major reforms by the occupation authorities does not mean that Japanese democratization was the product only of GHQ directives. The important players were not government authorities, who submitted only reluctantly to the GHQ policies, but rather the popular organizations and the overwhelming number of the people who enthusiastically embraced the reform measures. Many women wholeheartedly welcomed the directives calling for women's liberation; millions of independent and tenant farmers welcomed the land reform measures; small-

and medium-sized business and shop owners embraced the policy of *zaibatsu* dissolution and free competition; and many children and teachers welcomed the educational reforms and were eager to study new subjects. These people were the driving force behind the significant advances that Japan made after the reforms were introduced.

It cannot be said that the United States reformed Japan. GHQ simply provided Japan with the opportunity to carry out reforms. Their gift was the destruction of the obstacles that had stood in the way of reform. The Japanese people have not forgotten this great accomplishment. But the people who gave substance to the reform measures and turned them into reality were the reformers among the Japanese people—not the occupation authorities or the conservative government. They were, instead, those who experienced the terrible wartime and postwar crucible and developed a powerful will to endure and live, survived the ordeals, and worked strenously for the revival of Japan.

Chapter 2

THE LIFESTYLE REVOLUTION

THE WARTIME ECONOMIC SYSTEM

For the Japanese economy, Shōwa was a period of great turbulence, from the Great Depression and the wartime economy to Japan's defeat and the enormous damage and confusion that resulted. The subsequent economic revival of the occupation period and the high-speed growth that started in the second half of the 1950s made the period a stormy segment of history indeed. This chapter turns away from the larger economic changes, however, to focus instead on the history of Japan's "lifestyle revolution."

From the mid-1950s to the 1970s, the traditional Japanese way of life, an essentially agrarian existence that had continued unbroken from the Yayoi period (third century BC), was completely swept away. These changes were so enormous that, though unrelated to any shifts in political power, they constituted a revolution—a revolution in lifestyle.

The most drastic changes occurred in the 1960s, the pinnacle of the high growth. The decade included two major periods of great economic prosperity. The first was called the Iwato boom, because it was thought to be the greatest economic boom since the Iwato era, when the mythical sun goddess sealed herself in a cave behind a stone door. The second, the Izanagi boom, was similarly named for the even older age of the founding god, Izanagi. Real economic growth during these years exceeded ten percent annually. Of course, there were brief lapses like the so-called "bottom of the barrel" recession of the mid-1960s, but even including such periods of decline, actual economic growth averaged over ten percent, an incredible pace that lasted for twelve to thirteen years.

The doubling and tripling of Japan's economy during the high-growth years not only raised the national per-capita income many times over, it stimulated a mass migration of people from the rural to the urban areas.

Approximately ten million people moved from the farm villages to the cities. In the process, rapid lifestyle changes occurred, affecting modes of transportation and communication, the kind of goods consumed, the etiquette and ceremonies practiced in daily life, general social conditions and customs, and so on.

Japanese born during or after the lifestyle revolution take these changes for granted, but for people raised in Japan before the 1950s, the changes represent a major disjuncture. The unfolding of this major revolution in lifestyle, then, is the most significant characteristic of the Shōwa era. To reveal the inner nature of the time, let us review the historical events that led to the lifestyle revolution.

Shōwa history began in a time of economic crisis. Seeking to break out of the worldwide depression, Japan rejected the course pursued by the United States—that of turning inward to develop new resources, open up new markets, and stimulate domestic demand—in favor of the German and Italian strategy of invading other nations to acquire new territories. In the process of pulling out of the crisis, the Japanese economy underwent significant changes that contributed to the great economic advances it later achieved.

One such development was the Japanese capitalist shift to heavy industrial and chemical manufacturing in the 1930s, built around the defense industry. Of course, the steel and machine industries had existed before, but from the 1930s the ratio of heavy and chemical industries to light industrial production became much greater. The direct cause for this development was the growing defense industry. In order to prepare for war with the major powers, the state energetically promoted the building of industrial facilities and the capacity to produce iron, machinery, refined oil, airplanes, warships, motor vehicles, and so on. Thirty to forty percent of the national budget was devoted to the military. As a result, Japanese capitalism, previously at a very early stage of development, rose to the level of heavy industrial and chemical production.

New business complexes emerged in addition to the old *zaibatsu* such as Mitsubishi, Mitsui, Sumitomo, and Yasuda. These new industrial corporations went after markets overseas and developed industries primarily in Korea and Manchuria and also in Southeast Asia. Thus a pattern emerged in which the new bearers of the Japanese economy after the Shōwa economic crisis moved in conjunction with the military, which was advancing on the continent after the Manchurian Incident. This development became one of the underlying conditions for postwar Japan's rapid economic advancement.

The National Mobilization Law

Japan's recovery from the Shōwa economic crisis coincided with an up-surge in leftist political activity, including many labor and tenancy dis-putes. The frequency, intensity, and number of participants of these incidents increased, reaching a prewar high from 1935 to 1937. In the latter half of 1937 (after the Marco Polo Bridge Incident of July 7 that brought all-out war between Japan and China), these disputes were strongly sup-pressed by the government and dropped off rapidly. In retrospect, though, it is clear that the leaders of labor and tenancy disputes curtailed their ac-tivities not only because they feared the crackdown but because they shared the sense that a national crisis was facing Japan. Opposition parties like the Workers' and Farmers' Party (*Rōnōtō*) and the Social Mass Party (*Shakai Taishūtō*) also changed their stance and rushed to support the poli-cies of the military and the government. This phenomenon undoubtedly reflected the prevalent belief that national and state interests were more important than class interests.

In 1938, at the behest of the military, the National Mobilization Law was enacted limiting the free conduct of business activities. Industrial pro-duction in some sectors was restricted completely; other industries judged to be essential to defense production were provided with enormous amounts of state aid and expanded significantly. When there was a short-age of workers in these industries, the National Mobilization Law and the conscription decree were invoked to recruit people to work in the defense-related plants. Labor unions were forced to disband, and those who re-sisted were persecuted. With this law, economic fascism—what might be called national socialistic policies—made its appearance.

Citizens' lives were severely regulated under the National Mobilization Law. Basic necessities, in particular food and clothing, were rationed under a system implemented by neighborhood associations (*tonarigumi*), created as subunits of the city and ward governments. All aspects of daily life were under the control of the neighborhood associations. No one, even those who on principle objected to this system, could ignore the imperatives of the neighborhood associations if they wanted to receive food rations. As the war expanded and shortages of essential goods became more acute, military personnel, bureaucrats, and businessmen acquired consumer goods unfairly on the black market, while ordinary people without access to these means of obtaining goods became increasing desperate.

On the other hand, munitions plants, exceedingly well protected by the state, garnered huge profits. These companies were able to use workers who virtually had been forced to work at low wages, under the rationale that they were serving the nation. The materials necessary for production were provided to the plants by the military, and the government ensured that facilitating their work would receive top priority.

The law was also imposed in the farm villages, where farmers had to turn over their rice production to the government. A quota system was introduced, and farmers who failed to meet the assigned quota were penalized. In return, the government aided the farmers in many ways, including crop subsidies and a limit on the landlords' share of their tenants' rice and wheat crops, which previously had exceeded half of production. Without such a cap, the tenant farmers would have found it difficult to deliver the quota demanded by the government and productive capacity would have declined. These government limits on some of the benefits and rights of the landlords became a basis for the postwar land reforms.

Many of the bureaucrats in the Ministry of Agriculture and Forestry in the late 1930s were former leftists who had rejected politics and found their way into the government bureaucracy. They made clever use of the wartime economic controls to significantly curb the power of the landlords. For example, they changed the tenancy fee from a percentage of the harvest to cash payment. Moreover, the cash payment to landlords was set at a different amount than the price the government paid to farmers for rice and wheat. The price of the farmers' crops that were to be expropriated by the government was set higher than the price of crops to be sold to the landlords. Through these policies, the power of tenant farmers and independent farmers was strengthened during the war years without recourse to more radical, socialist policies. This concern for the farmers arose in part from Japan's experience that in wartime farm production dropped rapidly if the government ignored the farmers.

The reasoning behind these measures was quite simple: the exploitative landlord system had to be curtailed in order to keep the war machine working. In addition to the usual hardships, the universal wartime draft created a shortage of farm workers. Moreover, fertilizer, farm machinery, and other necessary goods disappeared, posing a serious threat to agricultural production and, thus, to the war economy as a whole. In order to sustain production, the people who engaged in farming had to be supported.

Thus when the GHQ called for land reform after the war, the bureaucrats in the Ministry of Agriculture and Forestry were able to respond readily with a radical plan. Naturally, the landlord alliance and the conservative party resisted their plan very strenuously.

Air Raid Damage and Disastrous Inflation

As the war situation worsened, beginning in the latter half of 1943, Japan's marine transportation system virtually collapsed as enemy forces attacked the merchant marine fleet. Essential supplies like oil from Indonesia, rubber and minerals from the Malay peninsula, iron ore from China, and other raw materials from the occupied territories no longer reached Japan. As these resources ran out, Japan's labor force also increasingly declined and the nation's productive capacity dropped. In addition, factories came under attack with the start of air raids in 1944. Many factories were moved into tunnels dug in the mountains, but even these areas came under attack. Consequently, from the latter half of 1944, Japanese economic strength declined rapidly and heavy industrial and chemical productivity dropped to below one-third of the 1943 peak.

Information about these developments reached the emperor. The following is from his *Soliloquy*:

> As for the situation regarding munitions production at home, the weaknesses were as follows: . . . a factory that used to produce fifty torpedoes could produce only one. . . . if we were to insist on producing the torpedoes needed by the navy, all the factories producing army weapons would have to be turned over to the navy. Given this situation, I believed that it was no longer possible to defend the nation.
>
> On this occasion Prince Higashikuni Moriatsu arrived and reported specifically on numerous affairs. I had been informed until then that the coastal defenses were in bad shape, but according to his report it was not just the coastal defense; the divisions reserved to engage in the decisive battle also did not have sufficient numbers of weapons. I was told that the iron from bomb fragments dropped by the enemy was being used to make shovels. This confirmed my opinion that we were no longer in a position to continue the war.

Government expenditures for 1941 amounted to 16.5 billion yen (about $4 billion). By 1944, a year before the end of the war, outlays had risen to 86.1 billion yen (about $21.5 billion)—a five-fold increase in the short space of three years. Of this amount, 73.5 billion yen, some eighty percent of the total budget, was devoted directly to military expenditures.

The rapid increase in budget outlays resulted in disastrous inflation. To deal with this situation, the government strengthened the price control system. But because a large amount of money was in circulation where there was a serious shortage of goods, inflation could not be curbed. Initially, the difference between black market prices and officially fixed prices was about one to five, but it quickly rose to one to ten, then one to one-hundred. By the end of the war, the difference rose to well over one to one-hundred. Government control of the economy collapsed. For the citizens who had to survive by the daily food rationing system, which fell below minimum calorie requirements, this breakdown was catastrophic for living conditions.

In 1943, the production of pig iron hit a peak of 7,650,000 tons. But by 1945 this had dropped to 560,000 tons—less than one-tenth the 1943 tonnage. This inability to supply the key material of munitions production was evidence that the situation had become hopeless. Japan also was virtually without oil. The government even tried to get people to gather strange things like pine tree root oil to use as an oil substitute, but of course such alternatives could not power airplanes. Japan was in a desperate state.

THE BREAKDOWN OF LIFE AFTER THE DEFEAT AND THE OCCUPATION REFORMS

Japan's defeat in the war began with the nation's descent into economic disintegration. In light of the terrible situation, the emperor's "noble decision" to end the war, though too late, was the only logical decision. When the occupation forces entered Japan, as a precursor to the reforms they adopted measures to make certain that the people would not starve to death. They brought a large amount of food from the United States that was ordinarily fed to domestic animals and distributed it for human consumption.

I, too, ate a lot of feed that was meant for cows, pigs, and chickens. Rice was supposed to be supplied by the government, but distribution was delayed and often no rice ration was provided. In the spring of 1946, I was discharged from the army and returned to Tokyo University. During this time, my landlady in Hongō where I had rented a room would often complain about the delays—sometimes up to forty days—in the rationing out of rice. In desperation, we dug up the university lawn and planted yams, which we divided among us and cooked—stems, roots, and all. On Sundays we searched for grasshoppers.

In those days, the farmers avoided turning over their rice harvest to the government; instead, they hid it so they could sell it at exorbitant market prices to city people who came in search of food. They also bartered rice for things that urbanites brought to exchange for food. Thus city dwellers were all thin, and anyone with a rounded belly or cheeks was suspected of having done something illegal to get food.

Photographs taken around 1944 and 1945 show adults stooped over from hunger on the roadside, near railroad stations, and against walls or fences. In the more serious cases they lay down, but if they lay down too long, they froze to death. For two to three years after 1945, such conditions also were prevalent in the big urban centers. The situation was partly the result of massive unemployment and the occupation authorities could not proceed toward democratic reforms without addressing the problem. Thus the occupation authorities fought starvation in Japan.

The Japanese who lived during those years probably are all grateful to the occupation authorities for supplying food, food which the U.S. military personnel referred to as "disposable supplies" or "disposable food." Fortunately, the U.S. harvest in 1946 was so abundant that American farmers had difficulty marketing it all. This surplus continued for two or three years, and people all over the world benefited greatly from this abundance.

Under these fortunate circumstances, the decrees for reforms were issued. The Japanese people responded positively, even to the extremely radical reform decrees. In particular, the dissolution of the *zaibatsu* and, later, land reform boosted the Japanese economy. Japan's swift economic growth would not have been possible without these two measures.

The New Deal Dream Comes to Japan

Why were the *zaibatsu* dissolved? During the war, the entire munitions industry was run by *zaibatsu* entrepreneurs. These included the airplane, shipbuilding, automobile manufacturing, chemical (which produced gunpowder), iron production and metallurgy, and machine industries—all run by *zaibatsu* groups like Sumitomo, Mitsubishi, Mitsui, Yasuda, and newly risen business conglomerates like Mori (later Shōwa Electric), Riken (scientific laboratories), Kawasaki (heavy industries), Japan Nitrogen Fertilizer (later Chisso), Nissan, and so on.

The small and medium-sized industries were destroyed by air raids and ultimately were incorporated into the major industrial conglomerates. During the war, companies involved in defense production increased in size, and all the others were weeded out. Consequently, according to GHQ, at the end of the war the four major *zaibatsu* units—that is, the long-established *zaibatsu*—controlled almost twenty-five percent of the entire Japanese economy. When the newly risen corporate trusts were added, nearly half of the Japanese economy was in the grip of the *zaibatsu*. It is estimated that before total war broke out with China in 1937 the four major *zaibatsu* shared about ten percent of the Japanese economy, so it is clear that the *zaibatsu* grew very rapidly in the wartime economy.

Because of the influence of the *zaibatsu*, GHQ immediately took forceful, compulsory steps to dissolve them. MPs went to the head offices of Mitsui, Mitsubishi, Sumitomo, and others, seized their stock certificates, and placed them under seal. Then the conglomerates were divided into smaller companies—in some cases over a hundred new firms per *zaibatsu*. The occupation authorities instituted policies that could not have been introduced without military power to back them up. They severed the relationship between financial capital and industrial capital that had been so vital to the power of the *zaibatsu*.

At the same time, GHQ enabled small and medium-sized enterprises, which until then could not do business outside the framework of the conglomerates, to compete on equal terms with the former *zaibatsu*. In particular, antimonopoly laws were enacted. Without these reforms, small factories like the Tokyo Telecommunications Engineering Corporation and the Honda Technical Center could not have developed into the world-famous companies Sony and Honda. At one time, Sony was located in a dingy, dirty two-story barracks. How a tiny factory like that developed into the Sony of today is an incredible story. Honda began as a small motorcycle shop. The conditions that enabled these small companies to boom were created by the radical surgery that dissolved the *zaibatsu*.

The same period (1946–1948) brought land reforms, which—very importantly—gave Japanese farmers the will to work again. If GHQ had not imposed land reform during the occupation period, Japan undoubtedly would not have the prosperity that it enjoys today. GHQ's aggressive implementation of the reforms was revolutionary.

Land reform could not have been accomplished by Japan's domestic authorities. The dominant political party, the conservatives, and the National Landowners' Association were violently opposed to the reform measures. Instead, the reform policies were pushed forward by a large group of New Dealers in the government section of GHQ. These people were able to effect reforms—of which dissolving the big corporate trusts and redistributing farmland were only two—that they could not have dreamed of advocating for the United States. As New Dealers, they brought a dream of democratic reform to Japan and fought to see their policies enacted.

Needless to say, distributing control of factories and farmlands was not enough to guarantee high-quality production work. Boosting the morale of ordinary workers was another area in which GHQ played an important part by fostering the rapid growth of labor unions. GHQ believed that democracy could not be established without a healthy labor union movement, and less than a year after the war, five milllion workers were organized.

GHQ officials also were convinced that educational reforms were essential for the total eradication of militarism in Japan. As a result, an American-style 6-3-3 educational system was introduced, along with a policy to enable as many students as possible to get a high school education. Prior to this, very few students attended what was known as *chūgakkō* (literally, "middle school," but in the prewar system *chūgakkō* lasted five years, the counterpart of high school).

Middle school students had been looked upon as part of a privileged elite, and when I enrolled in middle school my mother addressed me formally, "Henceforth, you must do your best because you are entering a school where the object is to prepare for your rise to the top of society as an outstanding person." My father and mother had only finished elementary school, so "moving up to middle school," as we said, meant that I was joining a select circle of people—at least, that was how we country people felt.

In one stroke, GHQ made junior high school attendance (the middle three years in the new system) compulsory. It was an epochal reform, and it immediately created a huge shortage of teachers around the country. In addition to the new junior high schools, a three-year senior high school system was instituted. This large-scale creation of junior and senior high schools, which previously had been extremely few, resulted in an educated workforce during the later period of economic growth. Because modern industries need above-average workers who can think logically on scientific and technical matters, these educational reforms had an important impact on the Japanese people.

Many other democratic measures were introduced to Japan as well. These included new safeguards for human rights, constitutional guarantees of civil rights (see Appendix for the provisions on the rights of the people), civil equality for women, and revision of the civil code to reform the patriarchal family system. All of these measures contributed to the swift economic growth soon to come.

Around 1948, however, the U.S. government, in response to the growing Cold War, began to change its political management of Japan, and the liberal reformers were driven out of GHQ and sent back to the United States. Though it appeared initially that the New Dealers' hopes for reforms in Japan would be stymied, the movement toward democracy was not totally reversed because the Japanese people continued the job that the Americans had started.

THE POSTWAR RECOVERY

Inflation was the most serious economic problem of the seven-year occupation period (1945–1952), when the average cost of necessary consumer goods rose twentyfold. If the skyrocketing inflation had not been controlled, economic recovery would have been impossible. Drastic measures were called for.

The Shoup Tax System

The Japanese government was incapable of dealing with the immediate postwar problem of inflation. In 1949, Joseph Dodge, a bank executive from Detroit, arrived as a special adviser to MacArthur and compelled the Japanese government to adopt a strong anti-inflationary policy known thereafter as the "Dodge line." He pressured Finance Minister Ikeda Hayato to balance the national budget, impose a deflationary policy (which included cutting off loans to smaller enterprises), and adopt a fixed currency exchange rate of 360 yen to the dollar. Though these measures imposed hardships on workers and the struggling small and medium-sized businesses, they set the stage for economic recovery.

A seven-man tax advisory mission headed by Carl S. Shoup, a Columbia University professor, also arrived in 1949 and recommended fundamental reforms in Japan's taxation system. Shoup's recommendations, such as direct national taxation, a progressive income tax, and a blue sheet tax filing system, have continued in principle to the present. General MacArthur agreed with these recommendations and advised Prime Minister Yoshida Shigeru to put them into effect. Under this system, upper-income earners were taxed as high as seventy-five percent, while lower-income earners were taxed lightly. It was a stringent tax system as far as the financial world of that period was concerned, but revenue acquired by this new system was then utilized for economic recovery.

In recent years, talk of the Shoup tax system has resurfaced. In 1989, Japan's ruling Liberal Democratic Party (LDP) drastically reduced corporate and direct tax rates—a move completely counter to the thinking of Professor Shoup. The Shoup tax system was implemented to correct the enormous gap between rich and poor at the time by reversing the flow of capital through the imposition of a direct, progressive national income tax. The LDP proposed to revise this system in order to level the tax burden. The tax rate on the rich was lowered to a fifty percent maximum, and a three percent consumer (value added) tax, which the poor had to pay as well, was instituted. It is troubling that these measures were introduced just when the gap between Japan's rich and poor had reached its widest level in the postwar years.

I opposed the Shoup tax reforms when they were introduced. After graduating from college, I first took a job as a teacher at a junior high school in a mountain village, but by the time of the Shoup reforms I had returned to Tokyo to work at the Democratic Chamber of Commerce. My assignment was to go to the tax office and negotiate taxes, primarily on behalf of small businesses. Though I had majored in history in college, I also had studied tax law and accounting. Believing that the Dodge and the Shoup tax system would destroy small and medium-sized businesses, I joined the demonstrators calling for the repeal of the Shoup system and actively spoke out against it. In retrospect, however, I realize that my behavior was based on ignorance and that the road of Japan's postwar recovery has followed a complex, zigzagging course.

During this period, GHQ put forth its "nine-point economic stabilization plan" and introduced various emergency measures. For example, it called for the transfer of national funds and resources for strategic use in essential industries. In order to deal with food shortages, an enormous amount of capital was granted to the Japan Nitrogen Fertilizer Company, and the Shōwa Electric Industry also received subsidies to ensure sufficient electrical power. Also in order to ensure the availability of energy sources, GHQ made a priority of distributing resources and capital to coal mining companies. Although at one point coal production had dropped below ten million tons, in the short period of five years it rose to fifty million tons. Of course, this success was achieved through the back-breaking effort of the coal miners, but GHQ revived the war-torn economy through its targeted distribution of resources and capital.

These surgical measures had many victims: numerous poorly managed small and medium-sized businesses went into bankruptcy and, as a result, many people committed suicide. But once these rough times had been weathered, inflation was controlled and the economy began to stabilize. However, Japan also benefited from the special procurements during the Korean War, referred to by some as a gift from heaven.

The Korean War, Automobiles, and a Farewell to Hard Times

In the year before the Korean War broke out in 1950, a firm known as the Toyota Motor Company, hanging on the brink of bankruptcy, dismissed 1,600 workers. After the outbreak of the Korean War, Toyota went all out manufacturing parts and repairing damage to cars, bulldozers, and trucks used by U.S. troops in Korea. Through its energetic wartime procurement activity, Toyota eliminated its deficits in a short time. Indeed, it has been estimated that they made a profit of about ten billion yen during the war. Toyota's success was also partly thanks to the government's Cooperative Finance Commission's suggestion that they separate their production and sales divisions, thus enabling coordination of potential demand based on market surveys and production plans.

In 1956, the number of passenger cars produced in Japan was a mere 32,000, in contrast to the 5,816,000 produced in the United States. The rise of the Japanese auto industry coincided with the beginning, around 1955, of the era of high-speed economic growth. The number of autos produced reached about 600,000 by 1961. The most spectacular growth, however, occurred between 1963 and 1973, when economic growth accelerated and production figures doubled and redoubled, reaching 11,600,000 per year by the end of that decade. This period of economic recovery enabled the Japanese to overcome the terrible conditions that prevailed at the end of the war. This accomplishment was not only because of internal factors but also because of external assistance and manna from heaven—the special procurements that accompanied the wars of Korea and Vietnam. The long period of deprivation and endurance following the war came to an end in the mid-1960s.

The first step in escaping from deprivation and hardship was increased food production. Clothing production revived next, and then electrical products. But food came first. The general public got relief from hunger by around 1950, thanks to aid from the United States and the revival of agricultural production in Japan.

As for clothing, people started wearing fancier apparel from about

1955, and interest in fashion shows grew as well. Young Japanese people today might be surprised to learn this, but in the 1950s women of high school age and above, almost without exception, had sewing machines and sewed their own and their children's clothes and all sorts of other things.

As a result, sewing machine makers like *Jya no Me* (Snake Eye) and Ricker reaped large profits, many dressmaking schools opened, and sewing machines became essential accoutrements for brides. These sewing machines were the old-fashioned, foot-operated kind; electric and zigzag machines were invented much later. The establishment of the sewing machine as a common fixture in most households ushered in the era of electrical home appliances. The household electrical appliance industry became the first propellant of Japan's high-speed economic growth.

THE ERA OF HIGH-SPEED ECONOMIC GROWTH

The Take-Off to the Economic Miracle

The high-speed economic growth era consisted of two phases. The first of these was the postwar recovery, which included the beginnings of the recovery and the onset of the take-off. The take-off, which marked a final break with the prewar system, lasted from 1955 until about 1961, when the movement opposed to the U.S.–Japan Security Treaty was most active. During the take-off, the makers of home electrical appliances, such as Matsushita (National and Panasonic brands), Hitachi, Sanyo, Sharp, Toshiba, and Sony, made spectacular advances. Sales of Matsushita products increased an amazing seven-fold from 1955 to 1960. And this was a time when people coveted the "three sacred treasures" (*sanshu no jingi*)—the washing machine, the refrigerator, and the television. This desire for consumer goods became a dynamic force of domestic demand, uplifting and propelling Japan forward as an industrial empire.

The second period of the high-growth era comprised the years of genuine economic growth. In the early years of this period, all the industrial sectors, not just household electrical appliance makers, raced to invest in new facilities. Led by the steel, automobile, and chemical industries, the Japanese economy entered an expanding production-reproduction period in which investments induced further investments. At its peak, the economy was growing by eighteen percent—an amazing performance. Economists refer to this period as a time of "miraculous growth." The postwar economic reforms had generated a dynamic new popular energy that pushed the economy forward. The Japanese people, having experienced several years of technical innovation and the beginning of a consumer revolution, now exerted a new power.

One of the goals of this period was to successfully stage the 1964 Olympics in Tokyo. In the same year, Japan declared that it wished to join the advanced nations of the world. Having recovered from the wounds of the war, Japan joined the eight-nation International Monetary Fund and the Organization for Economic Cooperation and Development, both organizations consisting of advanced Western nations. The same year, the new, safe, "bullet trains," the fastest trains in the world, began running on the new Tōkaidō-Sanyō line and the expressway between Tokyo and Nagoya was completed. Tokyo became a modern metropolis, having undergone a total renovation. For all these reasons, 1964, the year in which the Tokyo Olympics were held successfully, is symbolic of the early years of high-speed economic growth.

In the later years of the high-growth era, people's driving energy reached its limits. After ten years (including the take-off period), the era began to run its course. Many Japanese businesses were vulnerable. Because of the limitations of their own funds, they had overextended by borrowing capital from financial institutions. Some sectors, such as the shipbuilding industry, suffered particularly, and their weaknesses became visible in the stock market. The structural weaknesses and imbalances of an economy that had relied excessively on importing technical skills from abroad also came to the surface.

But there were several achievements in these later years. One was effective government involvement. The state's financial strength, buttressed by the Japanese people's very high rate of personal savings, was used to sustain economic growth by investment in public works and other projects. Keynesian statistical economics also became established in Japan, and bureaucrats dealing with the economy became adept at economic predictions, enabling them to regulate the economy and sustain its vitality through financial and monetary policies.

Another factor played an important role: special military procurements in connection with the Vietnam War. The United States was heavily involved in Vietnam from 1965 to 1973. In 1966 alone, the United States invested about five billion dollars in the war effort, and in a four-year period it invested roughly fifty billion dollars. An enormous amount of that money also began to flow into Japan.

Vietnam War Procurements and the Izanagi Boom

Special procurements during the Vietnam War lasted for about five years. The procurements business fueled the economy and came to Japan just when the exceptional economic growth powered by the people's energy was on the verge of decline. Vietnam War procurements far exceeded the procurements for the Korean War. With 550,000 U.S. troops mobilized for modern warfare, huge quantities of supplies, machinery, clothing, food, medicine, bombs, artillery shells, and so on were required. Instead of transporting all of these supplies from the United States across the Pacific Ocean, it was cheaper to purchase them from a nearby industrial nation—and Japan was the only such nation. Today South Korea, Taiwan, Malaysia, and others would be able to supply these materials, but at that time most of the procurements for these supplies were made in Japan.

The procurement business sustained level economic growth during the second stage of the high-growth period. The Izanagi boom—ostensibly the greatest economic boom since the god Izanagi descended to the plains of the southern Japanese island of Kyūshū—was also fueled by Prime Minister Satō Eisaku's capital investment policy. The Izanagi boom started when the United States began bombing North Vietnam in November 1965, but took off after the Tet Offensive in February 1968 and continued until the United States was driven out of Saigon.

Though the special procurements were less than half, or even one-third, of the goods produced by the entire Japanese economy, they nevertheless had an enormous impact. Aside from the direct transactions, the procurement business triggered other economic activity, thereby significantly stimulating Japan's economy. The companies that were involved in supplying the U.S. armed forces during the Vietnam War included almost all of the major firms, led by Mitsubishi Heavy Industries, Nissan, Toyota, Honda, Sony, Matsushita, Hitachi, Nittoku Metal Industries, Canon, and others.

During this period, Adam Smith's idea that economic growth is the source of societal well-being gained widespread favor in Japan, giving rise to what became called the worship of economic growth. There was little criticism of the idea of economic growth, even by opposition groups like the Japan Socialist Party. There was virtually a national consensus. Conventional wisdom held that with economic growth public welfare would improve, the environment would get better, the gap between the rich and the poor would shrink, and the entire nation would become affluent. The formula seemed ideal. Thus, those few who expressed doubts about the paradigm of high-speed economic growth were regarded as eccentrics who enjoyed opposing the existing order. Only later were they viewed as people of great foresight.

Doubts about Economic Growth

During the second stage of high-speed economic growth in the mid-1960s, when the economy was growing annually at a rate of over ten percent, people became aware of serious new problems, such as the conditions of those whom we might call castoffs of industry. These people had been abandoned in society's dark corners and excluded from the general prosperity. For example, during this period coal mines had been decimated and practically all the coal miners were unemployed, requiring government assistance. Some drifted into the urban centers as homeless outcasts. The workers at the bottom social layer who had been swept into the slums of Tokyo (especially the Sanya area), Osaka (Kamagasaki), and Yokohama (Kotobuki-chō) created new social problems. Thus serious contradictions in the era of economic prosperity began to surface and pose the first questions about the myth of high-speed economic growth.

At the same time, the population of the farm villages continued to thin, and the number of abandoned villages began to increase. Reckless development impaired environmental quality and the fierce competitiveness that had become normal made people exhausted and high strung. In this situation, young people began to rebel and question the value of economic growth. These people later formed groups involved in ecological causes or those critical of industrialization, or they joined the zenkyōtō (all-student joint struggle) movement that called for the dissolution of the universities. Women, excluded from and exploited by the capitalistic market and the patriarchal family system, started the feminist movement in 1970. It was the beginning of a new age.

Hippie-like attitudes that ran counter to the existing social consciousness spread among the young people. Folk songs and pop music also entered the country and had strong emotional impact. In the 1960s, Beatlemania came to Japan, and rock bands began to spring up like bamboo shoots after a heavy rain. These developments constituted a counterculture movement that also motivated many young people to engage in more constructive social efforts. They joined movements to support the victims of Minamata disease (industrial mercury poisoning that occurred in Kyūshū) and SMON, subacute myelo-opticoneuropathy, a nervous system disorder that struck thousands in the 1960s who had been treated with the antibiotic chinoform. Young people also flocked to the anti-Vietnam War movement.

The most dramatic outburst of this social turmoil was the battle that exploded in the universities. Those affected by the activities of the student activist organization *zenkyōtō* may have felt that it was a confused, chaotic movement without clear objectives. But seen in the longer view, this movement was an inevitable expression of skepticism about the modernization of Japan. Doubts about Japan's course did not surface during the first stage of high-speed growth, but they became a unique contributor to the second stage.

Oil Crisis and Recovery

Just as the mushrooming problems of growth encouraged the business community to rethink the value of high-speed growth, the "oil shock" hit. When the 1973 Middle East war caused the price of crude oil to skyrocket, the Japanese economy tumbled temporarily into negative growth. The business world at first was able to adjust without much difficulty, but the enormous credit accrued from their compensatory expenditures caused a superabundance of money, so prices continued to rise. This trend led to "stagflation"—rising prices while the economy was in a downturn. As a result, the Japanese economy entered a third stage, adjustment, during which growth was reduced to two to three percent per year.

The price of a barrel of crude oil, the lifeblood of the Japanese economy, had stood at $1.50 to $2 in 1950, but it jumped to $15 and then to $20 after the oil shock. Because Japan's economic growth had been totally dependent on cheap crude oil, people began to panic, fearing that Japan might go under. In this frenzied atmosphere, ecological concerns were the first to be discarded. People concluded that they could not afford to fuss over extraneous issues like the environment or compensating the victims of pollution. And the financial establishment and the bureaucrats of the Ministry of International Trade and Industry began trumpeting self-serving arguments that everything would be lost if crucial business enterprises collapsed.

The business world felt that the recession could be overcome only through rationalized management and high efficiency, high productivity, and large cost reductions. It asked the government to pour capital into the economy—that is, to increase the national debt by as much as necessary to fuel a recovery. As a result, the national debt increased to about twenty percent of the government budget as money was poured into public enterprises in order to stimulate the economy.

At the same time, business leaders appealed to the labor unions not to strike, arguing that the business world was one big family, a communal body in which everyone shared the same destiny. They actively sought "proposals" from workers on ways to absorb the economic losses caused by the high cost of oil, ways to reduce costs, and ways to improve technology. The response to Toyota's request for original ideas from the workplace at the end of 1976 brought in 20,000 submissions, and some eighty percent were adopted. It was an amazing example of labor–management cooperation, not another Stakhanovite movement (the failed 1930s Soviet attempt to enhance the economy through worker involvement). By adopting creative ideas submitted by the workers and making operational improvements, management not only curbed labor union opposition, it also found a way to surmount the economic crisis.

With labor and management working in unison, Japan strengthened its position in international competition, and Japanese goods, with improved quality control, rushed like a torrent into the markets of America and Europe. This situation, though referred to as low-speed growth, continued for about ten years. During this period, the *zenkyōtō* student movement, which had been aimed at rethinking the modern, collapsed.

The fourth stage of economic growth, starting about 1986, was based on *endaka*—the strong yen. There had been a strong yen period once before, in 1971, after the "Nixon shocks," when President Nixon abandoned the gold standard and imposed a ten percent surcharge on many imports into the United States. But the second *endaka* produced a greater decline in the dollar and a stronger rise in the yen than had developed after the Nixon shocks. The dollar–yen ratio, which had been about 1 to 260, dropped close to 1 to 120, roughly doubling the value of the yen in the international market and thus also doubling the financial power of Japanese with large assets. Big business, in particular, was then a formidable force in international competition.

Because of the sudden rise in the value of the yen, the export market's ability to compete declined and, for a short period, companies active primarily in the export trade suffered. But exporters were helped by the lower cost of imported raw materials. Also, by scaling back on work for the subcontractors and thereby turning them into sacrificial lambs, they overcame the problems resulting from the strong yen. As exporters regained the ability to compete and acquire foreign currency, Japan rapidly became rich, and the excess profits spilled over to benefit lower-level salaried workers and consumers. This period saw the outbreak of the second consumer revolution. However, this time consumption did not focus on long-lasting, essential consumer goods; instead, people sought "soft" articles—that is, brand name goods or luxury items with distinctive characteristics and high ancillary value. In other words, it was a period of conspicuous consumption.

At the same time, production took a strong leap forward thanks to new technological innovations brought about by advancements in microelectronics, computers, biotechnology, robot technology, and so on. A "resource" no longer was thought to be a natural resource. Information became the critical resource. The combination of these factors propelled the great prosperity of the last years of the Shōwa era. Between 1985 and 1990, the economic growth rate rose above five percent for the first time in a number of years, and Japan became an unchallenged economic giant, surpassing the United States in per capita GNP. Big business turned to foreign investment as a way of earning high return on the excess capital it had accumulated. Not only did multinational companies grow in size, but they began to purchase things like foreign companies, valuable art objects, and real estate.

As for the domestic economy, prices stabilized because the strong yen made raw materials and other imports cheaper. As a result, even though service costs rose, overall prices of goods remained stable and interest rates remained at their lowest level in history until 1989. In addition, the price of crude oil dropped, and because the industrialized nations had cut back on oil consumption since the oil crisis, there now was a steady oversupply. The economy enjoyed a triple advantage: low energy costs, stable prices, and cheap interest rates caused by a surplus of money.

But trade conflicts with other nations began to worsen and domestic land prices skyrocketed. In a short time, land prices in the hearts of the major cities jumped not two times, but five times and ten times. Banks began to accept this inflated real estate (as well as securities) as collateral for enormous loans to businesses that, in turn, engaged in land speculation and made enormous profits equal to their regular business income. This investment style became known as *zaiteku*. Thus people once again began to attach importance to class, but this time the distinction was between the propertied and unpropertied classes.

The end of this period of *zaiteku* came in 1989 with the big drop in the Tokyo stock market, when the Nikkei stock index suddenly dropped from 39,000 to 22,000 yen. It was a drastic collapse that finally ended the long period of *endaka* prosperity. This was also the year in which a new page in world history was written as *perestroika* swept the Soviet Union and Eastern Europe and a storm of democratization destroyed the Cold War.

THE LIFESTYLE REVOLUTION: A SOCIAL HISTORY

The 1960s, the glory years of high-speed economic growth and an important age in Japan's lifestyle revolution, deserve closer examination. Three concepts are key to understanding this age: the transportation revolution, the information revolution, and the emergence of a mass consumption society.

Though the bullet train and the jumbo jet were important in Japan's transportation revolution, the most significant development was the formation of the automobile society. By 1971, there were over 20,860,000 cars in Japan. Life without a car became unthinkable, and all aspects of everyday life felt the impact. (By the 1980s, however, well after the car-centered lifestyle had been established, international air travel became common, even for ordinary people. At present, one out of ten Japanese travel abroad. Though it remains to be seen what effect this trend will have, I believe that a more open-minded Japan is bound to emerge.)

The other development in the 1960s that dramatically changed lifestyle was a revolution in information, which started with the electronics-based discoveries in communications. The star of this revolution was not the proletariat but the computer, which was introduced to all sectors of society with incredible rapidity. It changed not only the lives of individuals throughout Japan, but the social system itself. Information was no longer regarded merely as transmitted knowledge and news—it became power, strength, and authority, and an industrial resource. Scientific discoveries that have given us useful products thus also fall under the umbrella of the information revolution.

The upheavals in Eastern Europe in 1989 clearly show that information is power. Transcending the classical Marxist theory of revolution, which holds that class conflict and economic discontent are the chief causes of revolutions, information poured across boundaries to encourage the democratic uprisings, outbursts of years of discontent that led to huge demonstrations and the overthrow of governments. This was what Lenin did not know: information is the most significant cause of revolutions. And so it was with Japan's revolution in lifestyles.

The period from the postwar years until roughly the beginning of the

1960s was known as the "electrification of mom," referring to the wide-spread accumulation of the "three sacred treasures": the television, the refrigerator, and the electric washing machine. These goods gave way to the "three Cs" of the 1970s: the color television, the car, and the cooler (air conditioner). When most Japanese had acquired these items, they began dreaming of a second house, and the catchphrase "my home-ism"—referring to the concentration on home improvement and the comforts of home life—became the rage.

Another development was the rapid increase in personal savings. The average household savings increased four-fold between 1965 and 1975, from 760,000 yen to 3,160,000 yen. (The current average is close to 10 million yen.) With prices remaining stable, purchasing power grew, enabling people to spend their money on things like foreign travel, brand-name goods, or luxuries like pianos. The average household income also jumped during this ten-year period, from 780,000 yen in 1965 to 2,900,000 yen in 1975. (Today it is over 6,000,000 yen.) These forces propelled the periods of immense economic growth, the three-and-a-half-year Iwato boom and the five-year Izanagi boom, and led to great changes in Japanese attitudes toward such things as clothing, food, sex, and housing.

Today the Japanese do not wear clothes to protect themselves from the elements; they do so to make themselves look beautiful, or because it gives them a sense of luxury, or because it gives them pleasure. The same is true of food: Japanese no longer eat to live. Today they all want to become gourmets. The emphasis in Japan today is on how to enjoy food and how to make food look beautiful so people can talk about it.

The same can be said about sex and gender issues. Today, sex is regarded as an important means of enabling people to enjoy life; it is no longer tied to marriage, reproduction, or love. Japan's male-centered society is being shaken, especially by women's positive affirmation of sexuality and their openness about sexual activity, together with their fundamental criticism of sexual discrimination. The enactment of the Equal Employment Opportunity Law of 1985, which banned sexual discrimination in the workplace, marked the full-scale advancement of women in society. Indeed, women were the moving force behind the lifestyle revolution.

In the area of housing, however, quality and quantity have remained low. The typical modern Japanese kitchen and living room, sought as amenities of modern life, were designed to be similar in size to the cramped housing provided in developments by public housing corporations and the government. Not only have the Japanese not been able to escape these cramped living quarters (rabbit hutches, as they've become known) but they cannot even hope to *obtain* them. A sense of hopelessness still prevails as far as housing is concerned.

But in contrast to Japan's urban centers, the outlying areas seem to offer a richer life. In places like rural Toyama prefecture, an average of seventy percent of the people own their own houses. But the income that sustains these houses usually does not come from traditional farms and businesses: the families often are dependent on income earned by family members who work away from the home community or on the money that housewives earn by working part-time at a nearby factory. Thus, many families have very little financial latitude.

Those Left Behind

In 1970, the Osaka International Exposition was held with great success. At that time, a reporter from the *Mainichi Shinbun* conducted an interview with Ishizaka Taizō, the chairman of the Japanese International Exposition Association. An excerpt from the interview follows (August 18, 1970):

> *Reporter:* Won't environmental pollution pose serious problems for business operations?
> *Ishizaka:* I have lived in Edo [Tokyo] for eighty years, but I have never felt any effects of pollution. No one has died of environmental pollution. It makes no sense to call for the prevention of environmental pollution at the cost of destroying industry.
> *Reporter:* But don't you think that environmental pollution has become extremely serious?
> *Ishizaka:* I don't think that's the case at all.

Ishizaka Taizō, a former president of the Keidanren (Federation of Economic Organizations), was the top figure in the financial–business world. Regardless of his words, many people had died and continue to die from pollution in Minamata (mercury poisoning), Toyama (cadmium poisoning), Niigata (mercury poisoning), Kawasaki (air pollution), Yokkaichi (air pollution), and other places. According to the *Asahi Shinbun* of July 30th in the same year, Prime Minister Satō is reported to have declared at the Conference of the National Prefectural Assembly Presidents that, "We cannot slacken the pace of economic growth just because of environmental pollution." Just when public anxiety about environmental pollution was reaching an unprecedented level, Japan's top government and business leaders showed an unforgivable lack of concern.

It appears that some Japanese entrepreneurs were unable to realize that unbridled production would deplete natural resources and eventually destroy the environment, including human life. And government leaders behaved in a similar fashion, seeming to think that toxic industrial waste would be decontaminated naturally by Japan's seas and rivers. Neither the central government nor the local administrative organs formulated any policies or provided any funds to take care of contaminated waste. They aggressively pushed reckless—here I do not call it high speed—economic growth for twenty years. Then the enormous costs of contamination suddenly appeared in the form of widespread environmental destruction: ruined mountains and rivers, thirty or forty thousand cases of pollution-related diseases, air pollution in the form of photochemical smog, and multiple contamination of the Inland Sea and the Shiranui Sea (from Minamata mercury poisoning, which killed over three hundred people and afflicted thousands).

While creating these problems, big businesses crushed weaker, smaller firms through relentless competition. Fishermen, who lost their fishing grounds, rapidly dropped in number, and farmers, who at one point in the early postwar years had constituted forty-four percent of the total working population of Japan, were reduced to nine percent by 1975.

In addition, a large number of social dropouts began to appear, forming the bottom layer of Japanese society. The dropouts were disabled people, the old, and those who had been used and abandoned in the course of economic development. The lifestyle revolution bears the heavy burden of the people who had been driven out of the marketplace, and when we evaluate the character of this period we must make this fact the central focal point.

I would like to conclude by looking at some of the main aspects of the lifestyle revolution in terms of social history. For Japan, the period was one of momentous, unprecedented changes. It was a revolution without a shift in political power, triggered by rapid economic development that brought modernization to every corner of Japanese society.

In the wake of the population shift from the rural areas to the cities, over eighty percent of the population now live in an urban environment and have been freed completely from the danger of starvation. In the twenty-year period from 1950 to 1970, labor productivity rose 10 times (while in the United States, it rose only 1.4 times). As the GNP soared from 13 trillion yen in 1960 to 200 trillion yen in 1980, the annual growth rate averaged over ten percent. Also, Japan quickly transformed into an information society, with the number of televisions increasing from one million in 1958 to ten million just four years later. Japan now has the highest life expectancy in the world. The vast majority of the people have considerable savings and own their own cars. Surveys indicate that Japanese people consider themselves to be middle class and that they generally are satisfied with their lives.

These developments, occurring in such a short period of time, quite naturally brought about significant changes and not a little confusion in people's lives. Traditional customs and practices also changed profoundly. But even though many of the old customs transformed during this period, the peoples' underlying sentiments and folk consciousness did not disappear. In the midst of the superficial trendiness are signs of the persistence of deeper, unchanged traditions. The relationship between the great changes of the period and the vestiges of tradition can be seen clearly in three areas: rites of passage, the information society, and crime. Examining these areas enables us to portray the social character of the time.

Rites of Passage

Rites of passage reflect society's attitude toward personal milestones. During the Shōwa period, the chief Japanese rite of passage ceremonies (birth, coming of age, marriage, sixtieth birthday, death, and memorials, among others) remained, but because Japanese lifestyles altered completely, these ceremonies also underwent important changes.

The breakup of the traditional household is one reason for changes in the rites of passage. Extended households, consisting of three generations (grandparents, parents, children), and even nonfamily members, have decreased drastically, and so traditional ceremonial practices are more difficult to pass on. The result has been confusion and a deterioration in the way these rites are conducted.

In the early years of Shōwa, the rites of passage were performed mainly in the home, but now most ceremonies are performed publicly. Also, people's ties to local community institutions have weakened, giving way to increased corporate participation in private ceremonies and to their commercialization. Regional, class, and occupational differences in the performance of rites of passage have virtually disappeared because of the spread of the information-based society and other lifestyle changes. Instead, new ceremonies (more like performances) for a modern consumer society have emerged. Also, the great increase in life expectancy has given people many years for which there are no traditional ceremonies. As a result, the concept of personal milestones has changed. And finally, Japanese have developed uncertainties toward their traditional conceptions of the soul and the afterlife.

It used to be said that the dead became spirits who rested peacefully in the hills or sea near their homes or in their graves. After the traditional thirty-three- and fifty-year memorial services were completed, the spirits turned into ancestral spirits who watched over still-living descendants. But today people question such beliefs, thanks to both the lifestyle revolution and the spread of a scientific worldview based on rational education. For these and various other reasons, Japanese today are losing their traditional belief in the other world—the spiritual world—and in the rebirth of spirits. The view is gradually spreading that the bodies and spirits of the deceased return to the land and eventually disappear into nothingness.

Formerly, mountain people, coastal dwellers, and those in the villages and towns all had their own rites that were rooted in the life of their particular region. Also, the various economic classes had their own forms of rites. As Yanagida Kunio, Japan's greatest folklorist, showed, at one time the ritual ceremonies of ordinary people were an intimate part of their lives. But since the 1960s these diverse practices have disappeared one after the other, and an urbanized, common lifestyle and sensibility have taken their place. We are currently in the midst of these drastic changes, and it remains to be seen when this leveling uniformity will cease or when the traditional pattern will revive.

But what, then, is the meaning of the recent revival of the worship of Kannon (the bodhisattva goddess of mercy) and Jizō (the bodhisattva protector of children) and the popularity of ceremonies for the souls of stillborn children and aborted fetuses, séances, astrology, psychics, and new religions? The steady leveling of lifestyles may be a surface phenomenon. Does this resurgence mean that traditional beliefs are deeply embedded in Japanese peoples' underlying consciousness and persist essentially without change? No. These beliefs are not simply the vestiges of old ways; rather, they may be a postmodern fusion of the old spirituality with the new social consciousness.

Information

The information society, often referred to as postindustrial society, has introduced intricate instruments into the workplace, from computerized production machinery to robots. As a result, the need for physical labor has been reduced drastically and people's concept of labor has changed completely. The reduction in physical labor seems to have eliminated the deeply etched shadows that once characterized Japanese expressions, but it also has removed the scent of the wind and soil and the feel and texture of nature from Japanese lives. In particular, children have been cut off from farm work and thus have been denied the chance to experience a deep relationship with nature. This change has significantly influenced personality formation, resulting, for example, in the emergence of the "homebody tribe," layabouts who are attached to their electronic toys. The burgeoning realm of vicarious experience based on television, video, and personal computers has resulted in a sham culture.

The computer, the main player of the infomation society, has revived the age of high-speed growth. The widespread and rapid expansion of computerized equipment in such areas as the national railroads, highway network, airline systems, and communications grid has drastically altered people's sense of time, space, and travel. Today, traveling is no longer an encounter with the unknown—now it is simply movement from one place to another. This attitude has arisen from the automobile society, which has dramatically expanded the perimeter of possible social circles and relationships.

The information society has eroded the world in which culture was transmitted by word of mouth. The nationwide diffusion of standard Japanese language has hindered the oral tradition in literature, especially folktales. Only some old *kataribe* (storytellers) have survived, like antiques from the past. Children and young people, who used to listen to their stories with rapt attention, now are absorbed in television. Moreover, new family systems have reduced grandparents' contact with their grandchildren. Thus, opportunities for passing on tradition are lost, leaving it in danger of disappearing. Scholars have been busily recording this cultural tradition before it is gone. Recently, however, signs of revival have appeared from a different direction and some positive aspects of the information society have surfaced.

One positive sign in the relationship between the information society and mass culture is the phenomenon known as *karaoke*. (Literally "empty orchestra," karaoke machines play only the background music of popular and folk songs, allowing individuals to sing the vocal parts.) About ten million high-tech karaoke machines, some even equipped with laser disc videos (and subtitled lyrics), are located in clubs, bars, hotels, restaurants, private party rental rooms, public halls, and even in ordinary family homes throughout Japan. Karaoke has become one of Japan's most popular recreations. Singing *enka* music (Japan's equivalent of sentimental country and western) is the most common form of this narcissistic activity, but the other force behind the karaoke boom is its expression of an undercurrent of traditional sentiment. *Enka* songs, which mainly concern love, have stubbornly survived the storms of the lifestyle revolution and the information society. *Enka* seems to share many of the qualities of the Korean "songs of sorrow," and, indeed, this type of music may reflect the deep-seated shared consciousness of the Japanese and Korean people.

Information is now the lifeblood and nervous system of contemporary society. It has transcended the bounds of race and nation and become truly global. Information is even changing the framework of our thought, which once viewed information as permanent and unchanging. The ways in which information is conveyed have also changed. People now get their intellectual messages from screen images rather than printed letters and from performance rather than words.

Crime

Crime also has been profoundly affected by information. Certain crimes could not have been committed outside the context of the information society. These are exemplified by some infamous crimes in Japan during the 1970s and 1980s—widely-discussed cases that shocked the nation and dominated the mass media. Though these crimes reflect the greed and desires of people struggling at the bottom layer of Japanese society, they struck a chord with the general public and evoked a strong reaction in the popular consciousness.

The first examples involve politically motivated crimes: the "Wolf Pack" case, which threatened Japanese big business in 1974, and the major incident involving the "twenty-one-faced monsters" in 1984. Another group of crimes were committed by youths, including the death of a third-generation Korean–Japanese boy who was taunted at school, a boy's brutal murder of his parents with an aluminum bat, the serial murders of drifters, and the kidnapping and murder of young girls by a boy known as "M-kun" (Master M). These crimes have become symbols of a new age for the Japanese.

The chief actors in the first crime, the Wolf Pack, were several anarchists who claimed to be members of the East Asian Anti-Japanese Remilitarization Front. They bombed several large corporations, including the headquarters of Mitsubishi Heavy Industries, where 8 people were killed and 165 were wounded. The second crime was committed by a group nicknamed the Twenty-One-Faced Monsters because they wore masks that resembled the Twenty-Faced Phantom, a character from a popular 1940s comic book. They blackmailed the Morinaga Corporation, the largest confectionery manufacturer in Japan. They have never been caught. Both of these criminal gangs inflicted serious blows against firms that were representative of big business, though the type of crime was completely different in each case. Yet, as examples of crimes committed in the information society, they are very contrasting in terms of strategy and tactics, media image, and popular perception.

The popular image of the Wolf Pack and the Monsters was completely different. The Wolf Pack was feared and hated, while the Monsters were applauded by the public. The Wolf Pack sought to form a common front with the Ainu and Okinawan minorities, who suffered social discrimination within Japan, and with the people of Korea, China, and Taiwan, who had been victims of overseas Japanese aggression. The Wolves struck at big business intellectually and tactically by carrying out frontal attacks intended to destroy Japanese imperialism. The Monsters, on the other hand, mocked the police and the business world and used guerrilla tactics—terrorizing corporate confectioners by surreptitiously mixing potassium cyanide into candies and then announcing publicly what they had done.

The decisive difference between these groups lies in the contrasting ways in which they dealt with information. The Wolf Pack endeavored to cut themselves off completely from the information media. They acted under complete secrecy as terrorists. As a result, those in power were able to monopolize information to make public opinion their ally and to depict the terrorists as thoroughly sinister criminals. Finally, by combing through apartments, the police arrested the entire Wolf Pack. Their ideals of anti-imperialist struggle and their call for East Asians to rise up against Japan ultimately failed to reach the public.

Though these terrorists were disposed of ignominiously in the end, their crime did not lack drama. The bombing of Mitsubishi Heavy Industries was staged on August 30th, a day of protest against the oppression of Koreans residing in Japan. It is said that the powerful bomb they used had been manufactured to destroy a train transporting the emperor over the Arakawa bridge. The original plan had been to blow up the bridge in the exact fashion in which the bridge was blown up in *The Bridge on the River*

Kwai. However, because of the Wolf Pack's ignorance of the importance of the media—of information—they failed to advertise the dramatic features of their plan.

The Twenty-One-Faced Monsters, on the other hand, must have learned from the failures of the Wolf Pack. They thoroughly used the mass media to broaden the information battlefront. For over a year they mocked the authorities and apparently extorted a large amount of money from corporations. The criminals dramatized their actions while portraying themselves as righteous bandits. The Monsters caught the public imagination by railing against the industrial crimes of the Morinaga Corporation, which had caused the infamous Morinaga Powdered Milk Incident (a major case of arsenic poisoning in 1955, which affected 12,000 infants and killed 130) by using a cheap additive in its powdered milk. The Monsters then drew public fascination by directing the Fujiya Confectionary Corporation to throw 100 million yen in currency from the rooftop of their building. The group also called attention to themselves by sending some twenty-five messages of defiance to the police and the mass media. They made a complete mockery of the authorities by tricking the investigators and exposing the inept internal affairs of the police.

The Monsters struck at the weak point of big business—the means of disseminating mass sales propaganda in the information society. They very cleverly and effectively used information in contemporary society. While these criminals can be said to have taken the people hostage by spreading poisoned food, they meticulously made sure that the general public would not be harmed by publicizing their plan to poison certain products in advance. This tactic enabled people to relax and become spectators of this theatrical crime. At this point, crime had become entertainment.

The first example from the next group of crimes involves the brutal bullying in school that drove a third-generation Korean–Japanese, Yim Hyeon-Yil, to suicide in 1979. This first-year junior high school student was mocked, kicked, and abused by his classmates. Incidents of bullying and physical violence in the schools had been breaking out frequently throughout the country at the time. (The peak year was 1982, when there were 3,042 reported acts of violence committed against students at school and 1,563 reported attacks on teachers.) Yim was taunted with the common racial epithets and insulting stereotypes that Koreans endure in Japan. These discriminatory concepts must have been deeply embedded in the minds of the parents of his tormentors.

The second example, the "aluminum bat murder," occurred the following year in the home of a corporate executive in the city of Kawasaki.

The unemployed son, who was going to a preparatory school to retake his college entrance exam, brutally beat his sleeping parents to death with an aluminum bat because they had criticized him for misbehaving. This is just one example of a supposedly harmless young man who turned violent at home. Several youths were found guilty of killing and attacking their grandparents and parents in a number of incidents in 1980. After this incident, the term "aluminum bat" became a depressing symbol of the intimidation of parents by their children. It frightened parents whose sons were marking time to take college entrance exams. (The 1982 film *Family Game,* starring Matsuda Yūsaku, parodies this tragedy.) Another incident, in which the son of a well-to-do family (whose grandfather and father were both emeritus professors of Tokyo University) brutally murdered his grandfather, also shook the confidence of parents.

The third example from this group of crimes, dating from around 1983, involved boys who were rejected at home and at school as "delinquents" and "drop outs." They then went out in the streets to commit sinister crimes against weaker members of society. Ten students of a Yokohama junior high school formed a gang and attacked a number of homeless people, beating to death three people and inflicting serious injuries on more than a dozen people. When these youths' backgrounds were checked, it turned out that seven out of ten had come from broken homes. They had suffered psychological injuries and had dropped out of school or had run away from home, only to brutalize the weaker members of society who also had dropped out. Here, too, we see the dark forces at the bottom of contemporary Japanese society, and the hollowness of Japan's affluence and so-called democratic education system.

The shocking behavior of "M-kun" illustrates what can happen to someone who grew up as an outsider, even though he reached adulthood without committing the type of amoral actions taken by the youths discussed previously. One of the homebody tribe, as the growing number of youths obsessed with their personal computers and videos are called, M-kun isolated himself in his room (where he kept some 6,000 videocassettes). An introverted young man in his late twenties, he lived in a delusional fantasy world. He murdered a number of girls, most around five or six years old, and then took videos of them. The news of these hideous crimes sent shock waves around the nation. M-kun also vented his sense of rejection on the weak—in this case, the children who were his victims.

Moreover, it is symbolic that M-kun secretly had been practicing a traditional folk ceremony of the dead. In the ceremony of becoming one with the departed, he chewed the bones of his beloved deceased grandfather. Alone in his room, M-kun bound a candle on his head with a white towel and walked in a circle, a ritual practice intended to revive his grandfather. It is said that M-kun performed the same ritual for the young girls he had killed.

The deformed love that M-kun showed for his victims' corpses reflects not only a twisted sexual desire and masochism but also the revival of ancient customs. This case grotesquely illustrates the union of modern electronic technology and ancient folk ritual. As such, M-kun's crime is perhaps an emblem of postmodern crime, and it raises important questions about modern Japan.

Chapter 3

THE EMPEROR AND
THE PEOPLE

THE PERSONAL EXPERIENCES OF
THE SHŌWA EMPEROR

Hirohito was a record-breaking emperor; in all of Japanese history no other emperor either set or broke so many precedents. In Japan, three emperors are regarded as having taken decisive, epoch-making action: Tenchi (626–671), who established the ancient imperial state; Godaigo (1288–1339), who sought to impose direct imperial rule with the Kenmu Restoration; and Meiji (1852–1912), who reigned after the Meiji Restoration, when imperial rule replaced the feudal shōgunate. However, Hirohito, the Shōwa emperor, has greater significance than any of these.

Hirohito's sixty-four years on the throne is the longest imperial reign ever and in that time he weathered several major historical upheavals. Under Hirohito's banner, Japan went from being one of the world's top three military powers before the war to utter desolation with defeat and then rapidly rose to its place today as one of the world's top economic powers.

During Hirohito's reign, reliable information from around the world became easily accessible for the first time. No Japanese leader in history could match his level of access to information of all kinds. He outlived all the luminaries of his time—Roosevelt, Churchill, Hitler, Stalin, Mao Zedong, Chiang Kai-shek, Nehru—to emerge as a historical giant, a rich subject for historians. He could have made a great contribution to the world if he had retired to a quiet place and written his memoirs in a leisurely fashion. Unfortunately, his sudden terminal illness took away any such opportunity.

71

Education of the Young Prince

The Shōwa emperor, Hirohito, was born on April 29, 1901, making him quite literally a child of the twentieth century. He was the eldest son of the then-crown prince, Yoshihito, and he was given the name Michi-no-miya, meaning "the prince who leads."

According to the wishes of his grandfather, the Meiji emperor, the young prince was turned over to the family of Vice-Admiral Kawamura Sumiyoshi as soon he was born, and he spent the first four years of his childhood there. The Meiji emperor had many children, but several died at an early age and the emperor probably feared that children could not survive in the imperial court. Consequently, he decided to have Kawamura, one of his most trusted advisers, raise the baby Michi-no-miya. In this case, the emperor was especially concerned because Michi-no-miya was in line to become crown prince after his father became emperor.

When Vice-Admiral Kawamura died, the prince was turned over to an imperial household counselor, Marquis Kido Takamasa. The marquis was assigned the task of educating the prince, and his son, Kido Kōichi, became the prince's playmate. Kido Kōichi later became lord privy seal, the Shōwa emperor's most trusted adviser, and was constantly at his side during the war.

At age seven, Michi-no-miya entered the Peers' School, under the guidance of headmaster General Nogi Maresuke, the famous hero of the Russo-Japanese War of 1904–1905. When the Meiji emperor died in 1912, General Nogi committed suicide (to "join the Meiji emperor in death"), and he was succeeded by another hero of that war, a man called a "military god," Admiral Tōgō Heihachirō. The prince then received special instruction on imperial leadership at the Peers' School, with Admiral Tōgō as headmaster. Hirohito's later ability, as commander-in-chief, to scold and command military men was based on his experiences under General Nogi and Admiral Tōgō.

While Tōgō Heihachirō was in charge of the prince's education, the prince's instructor in the humanities for seven years was a man named Sugiura Jūgō. The contents of Sugiura's teaching up to 1918 was later published in the 1200–page volume *Rinri Goshinkō Sōan (Draft of the Ethics Lectures.* *

For someone preparing to become a national leader during the twentieth century, Michi-no-miya received an extremely narrow education. For

*Sugiura Jūgō, *Rinri Goshinkō Sōan* (Tokyo: Daiichi Shobō, 1936).

example, instruction in Japanese history centered heavily on the imperial court, and the remainder of his historical studies were mainly of Chinese history, starting with the third-century classic *History of the Three Kingdoms (Sanguo-Zhi)* and Confucian studies. European history and geography were also taught, but these lessons were less frequent. If the crown prince had been educated by international-minded intellectuals—men of the caliber of Mori Ōgai (1862–1922, renowned novelist and physician), Uchimura Kanzō (1885–1959, Christian leader), Minakata Kumakusu (1867–1941, anthropologist, archaeologist, and botanist), Yoshino Sakuzō (1878–1933, political thinker and advocate of democracy), and Nitobe Inazō (1862–1933, educator and Christian pacifist)—later affairs might have transpired quite differently.

Sugiura Jūgō was not the young prince's only lecturer, but it appears that he was the chief instructor in charge of the humanities. As a typical nationalist, he taught as historical facts the *Kojiki* (the *Record of Ancient Matters,* compiled in 712) the *Nihon Shoki* (the *Chronicles of Japan,* compiled in 720) and other mythical accounts of the age of the gods. In seven years as royal instructor, Sugiura devoted the vast majority of his over two hundred lectures to instruction in Confucian morality. Apparently, he cited examples from other countries only about thirty times.

In 1921, when the crown prince was twenty years old, he took a trip to Europe following the recommendations of Prime Minister Hara Kei and the aged advisor Saionji Kinmochi. There he reconsidered what he had been taught. In a much written about aspect of the trip, Hirohito was deeply impressed by two experiences in particular. One was meeting the British royal family and observing with shock the relatively free and intimate relationship they had with the citizenry. The prince decided that he, too, would like to establish that kind of relationship with the people of Japan. In a letter to his brother, Prince Chichibu, who went to study in England soon afterward, Hirohito wrote, "I discovered freedom for the first time in England. You, too, should enjoy the life of freedom there."

The other shock occurred when Japanese military attachés at the Paris embassy took the prince on a tour of the fortresses at Verdun, the site of the biggest battles between the French and German forces during the First World War. So soon after the war, the evidence of the destruction of Verdun was plain. According to his attendants, the crown prince expressed his opinion that a modern war should never be fought again. This site made a deep impression on the crown prince.

The crown prince returned from his travels on September 2, 1921.

Unfortunately, his stay in England lasted only four months; he was unable to converse in English, and a great deal of time was taken up by formal ceremonies. Apparently he didn't stay long enough to fully learn to question the biased worldview instilled in him by teachers like Sugiura Jūgō. Still, after tasting the freedom of the European world, he ventured out to the fashionable Ginza district with his friends from the Peers' School. Wearing a suit and tie, the young prince enjoyed the atmosphere with the people at the heart of Tokyo, then emerging as a modern city.

This was an era of worldwide arms reduction. In 1921, the United States proposed to Japan, England, France, and Italy that a conference be held in Washington to discuss arms limitation and problems related to the Pacific region and the Far East. The Japanese government appointed Katō Tomosaburō and Shidehara Kijūrō to attend the conference as plenipotentiaries. On November 4 of the same year, Prime Minister Hara Kei was assassinated in front of Tokyo station. Three weeks after this shocking experience, Crown Prince Hirohito was appointed regent.

Even after becoming regent, Hirohito was able to enjoy some degree of freedom. But this lifestyle ended suddenly with the assassination attempt known as the Toranomon Incident. In December 1923, shortly following the Great Kantō Earthquake, Nanba Taisuke, a son of a Diet member, ran up to the window of Hirohito's car and shot at him with a rifle. Luckily, the rifle was old-fashioned, and the bullet ricocheted off the roof of his car. As a result of this incident, however, the imperial family came under strict guard and could no longer go out freely. The prince was forced into the life of a "caged bird."

Turbulent Beginnings

Hirohito became Japan's 124th emperor on December 25, 1926, the day his father, the Taishō emperor, passed away. The *Gotaiten* (the official enthronement ceremony) and the *Daijōsai* (a ceremony of thanks to the sun goddess and other Shintō gods) took place two years later, in the fall of 1928. The actual date on which the crown prince took office as emperor, though, was December 25, 1926, and so, according to the system of calculating reign-years, year one of the Shōwa era consisted of only one week.

· The young emperor ascended to the throne in an extremely tumultuous era. A military confrontation with China broke out almost immediately. Japanese troops landed in China's Shandong province twice and at one point Japan occupied the Shandong peninsula. In May 1928, Japanese troops engaged the Chinese Nationalist troops in the city of Jinan (the Jinan Incident) and the bombing death of Zhang Zuolin (the warlord of Manchuria) occurred one month after this incident. Also, the bank crisis in March 1927 set off financial panic in Japan. Thus, from its beginning the Shōwa era was a time of serious social uncertainty in Japan. The start of Emperor Hirohito's reign did not presage a fortunate future.

Hirohito had acted as regent for the ailing Taishō emperor for a number of years and performed the duties of emperor; thus, he had some political experience before he ascended to the throne. Even though he was a new emperor, he could not be manipulated easily by the militarists and politicians because of his personal familiarity with the generals and political leaders. Indeed, the young emperor's independence can be seen in his response to the bombing death of Zhang Zuolin.

Zhang was the most powerful warlord in Manchuria at the time of his death. The involvement of Japanese Kwantung Army officers in the incident, without the knowledge of the government, provoked a serious crisis in foreign affairs: not only was this a violent act, but it impinged on the emperor's sovereign authority.

The emperor was extremely displeased that such a serious incident had been staged without his knowledge. He urged the prime minister, General Tanaka Giichi, a member of the Seiyūkai party, to make sure that the guilty persons would be severely punished. Tanaka promised the emperor that those responsible would be punished, and the army's investigation quickly implicated Colonel Kōmoto Daisaku. But key army officers, politicians of the Seiyūkai, and other right-wingers defended Kōmoto and opposed any punishment. Prime Minister Tanaka then tried to defuse the situation by forcing the commanding general of the Kwantung Army to retire and suspending Kōmoto. One year after the incident, in July 1929, he reported these measures to the emperor.

The emperor was enraged by Tanaka's handling of the affair. Tanaka tried to defend himself, but the emperor said, "I have no wish to hear your explanation" and left the room. This exchange led to the resignation of the Tanaka cabinet and the subsequent reappointment of Shidehara Kijūrō (who had been foreign minister from June 1924 to April 1927) as foreign minister. Shidehara immediately pursued a "revision" of the government's policy toward China and abandoned Tanaka's hard-line policy in favor of one of cooperation with the United States and Great Britain.

Despite the emperor's forceful actions, he was told (incorrectly, according to the law) by his aged advisor Prince Saionji that his response had interfered with the smooth operation of the Meiji Constitution. Later the emperor is said to have confessed that he had made a mistake, a youthful indiscretion, but it is questionable whether he really had done so. Although the ministers of the army and navy were part of the cabinet at that time, they primarily dealt with the military budget, personnel, education, and administration. These ministers had no direct military authority, which was held by the chiefs of staff of the army and navy, and the ultimate decision-making authority resided with the emperor. This dual system had been established by the Meiji Constitution.

Thus, it was natural for the emperor to insist, as the commander-in-chief of the armed forces, that military discipline be enforced strictly in the the case of the assassination of Zhang Zuolin. Prince Saionji told the emperor that he would cause a constitutional problem by refusing to accept the cabinet's decision. In retrospect, however, it seems that Saionji made a serious mistake: if his reproach led the emperor to be bound by this formalistic theory of constitutional monarchy, then it was also responsible for the grave misfortune that later beset Japan. As a result of the emperor's "self-reflection," the unjustly light punishment of Kōmoto Daisaku and other murderers was allowed to stand, and some elements of the military began to believe that the imperial command could be ignored. This perception was one of the causes of the military's arbitrary, self-willed, and illegal actions, which soon dragged Japan into the quagmire of war.

The emperor summarized his opinions of this affair in his *Soliloquy:*

The chief designer of this incident was Colonel Kōmoto Daisaku. Initially, Prime Minister Tanaka [Giichi] told me that he deeply regretted this incident. "This is only my personal opinion but because he killed the chief authority of the region I shall punish Kōmoto, and extend our regrets to China." This is what he said. . . .

But when Tanaka presented his proposal to punish Kōmoto to the cabinet, Transportation Minister Ogawa Heikichi argued vigorously that from Japan's standpoint it would be disadvantageous to impose any punishment. As a result, the cabinet vacillated and did nothing.

Thereupon Tanaka came to me once more and told me that he wanted to let the matter rest without taking any decisive measures. This was quite different from what he had told me earlier. So I told Tanaka in a firm tone of voice, "This is not what you told me earlier. How would it be if you resigned?"

Today I feel that it was my youthful spirit that made me talk to him the way I did. At any rate, that's what I said. As a result, Tanaka submitted his resignation and the entire Tanaka cabinet joined him. I hear that it was decided not to try Kōmoto in military court because he said that if he were interrogated in military court he would completely expose Japan's plot. . . .

After this incident I decided to sanction whatever the cabinet presented to me even if I did not agree with it.

This kind of self-reflection is repeated often in the *Soliloquy*. In this case, it is significant that the single sentence, "How would it be if you resigned?" brought down the cabinet. It is an important example of the absolute force of the emperor's authority.

Arrogation of Authority by the Army

The following year, 1930, Ishiwara Kanji, staff officer of the Kwantung Army, devised the plan for the military occupation of Manchuria and submitted it to the Army General Staff Headquarters. Of course, the plan did not propose immediate action by the military but was devised, it is said, to block the southward movement of the Soviet Union and communism. The emperor undoubtedly saw this proposal. The plan was implemented on September 18, 1931, when the South Manchurian Railroad was bombed outside the city of Mukden. The Japanese officers of the Kwantung Army said the action was undertaken by Chinese "bandits," but the officers had perpetrated it themselves to create an excuse to take over Manchuria.

On this occasion, there were several violations of the emperor's supreme command. In accordance with the wishes of Ishiwara Kanji and other planners, the commander of the Kwantung Army, Honjō Shigeru, ordered a general offensive and occupied all of Manchuria on his own authority. Even though the emperor had been presented with the plan, he had not specifically approved it. Another violation was by the commander of the forces stationed in Korea, General Hayashi Senjūrō. Upon receiving the request of the Kwantung Army, he sent bombers across the border to Mukden without the permission of the emperor, and he also independently sanctioned one brigade to cross the border into Manchuria.

These incidents were serious arrogations of imperial authority. Though the proper procedure required the army chief of staff to request permission from the commander-in-chief to initiate these actions, he deliberately did not do so. Later, Hayashi Senjūrō earned the tag "the general who crossed the border" and his arbitrary, high-handed actions were praised by military officials.

The Wakatsuki cabinet accepted the actions of the military forces in

Manchuria after the fact, but declared a nonextension policy that forbade the seizure of any more territory and the initiation of new hostilities. But Ishiwara Kanji ordered the bombing of Jinzhou on October 8, resulting in the international condemnation and isolation of Japan. The League of Nations established a committee to investigate the incident and soon after dispatched the Lytton Commission to Manchuria. But the emperor did not take any decisive action against the successive violations of his supreme command, and justified his behavior in the following manner:

> [I]n the instance of the Lytton Report [the League of Nations report is-
> sued at the time of the Manchurian Incident of 1931] I was prepared
> to accept the report and end the incident. I consulted Makino
> [Nobuaki, then lord keeper of the privy seal] and Saionji. Makino
> agreed with me but Saionji said it would cause difficulties if I were to
> oppose the cabinet's decision to reject the report. That is why I decided
> not to insist on having my way. In the case of Tanaka I did not veto his
> actions when I asked him if he should resign, I only advised him. But
> since then I decided that I would express my views on cabinet deci-
> sions, but I would not veto anything.

The emperor not only failed to punish Hayashi, the commander of the army in Korea who had usurped the authority of the high command, he also contradicted the preceding statement by presenting a commendation to the man directly responsible for the Manchurian Incident, General Honjō Shigeru. (The commendation stated, "You kept the masses under control with a few troops, and thus enhanced the prestige of the imperial army at home and abroad. I greatly rejoice in your unswerving loyalty.") Soon after, in 1935, General Honjō was received at the imperial court as the emperor's close adviser in the capacity of chief aide-de-camp.

The Kwantung Army took advantage of this situation and pursued Chinese guerrilla forces across the Great Wall and into China itself. On this occasion, however, the emperor justly condemned the action (his reproof is mentioned in the Honjō diary) and thereby averted certain war in China.

Another example of how the emperor began to lose confidence in the military is his *Poem of Eulogy for General Shirakawa Yoshinori*. During the Shanghai Incident of 1932, General Shirakawa, the commander of the Shanghai expeditionary forces, restrained the hard-line advocates of the general staff and ordered a ceasefire, thus limiting the fighting at Shanghai. Shortly thereafter, General Shirakawa was killed by a bomb thrown at him while he was reviewing the troops.

Upon hearing this news, the emperor deplored Shirakawa's death, saying, "Shirakawa had faithfully obeyed my command and just as I wished, he ended the fighting." He then composed a poem lamenting the general's death and sent it to the general's wife, Shirakawa Tama. The poem, which was transcribed in *Kido Kōichi Nikki* (*The Diary of Kido Kōichi*), reads:

> On the day of the festival of dolls
> for little girls, he ended the fighting
> I recall his heroic action*

In his recollections, the emperor states:

It was General Shirakawa's great achievement that he was able to limit the combat zone to the extent he did, and prevent the extension of the incident. The cease fire was achieved on March 3. This was not based on the issuance of an imperial command. I had asked Shirakawa before the fighting broke out to restrict the fighting. Because of his actions Shirakawa was criticized by the chief of the general staff [Prince Kan'in]. Upon Shirakawa's death I composed a poem praising the general's heroic achievement and sent it to his widow.

Thus, while he honored General Shirakawa in this manner, the emperor also had tacitly approved the arbitrary, independent actions of the generals who violated the borders of Korea and China and had honored the commanding general who had, without permission, launched an all-out invasion of Manchuria. After the war, this kind of contradictory behavior was exhaustively investigated for the war crimes tribunal by American attorney and prosecutor, Henry A. Sackett, when he questioned Kido Kōichi.

The complete translation of this interrogation has been published recently as *Kido Kōichi Jinmon Shirabesho* (*Documents on the Interrogation of Kido Kōichi*)[†] and is in the collection of historical documents on the Japanese occupation in the National Archives in Washington, D.C. Kido was a valuable witness to events of the time because he was lord keeper of the privy seal and a key advisor to the emperor during the crucial years from 1940 to 1945. Thanks to the efforts of Professor Awaya Kentarō and other historians who went there, made copies of the documents, and translated them into Japanese, the interrogation documents are available to Japanese historians. Compared to *The Diary of Kido Kōichi*, which is full of distor-

---

*Kido Kōichi Nikki, 2 vols. (Tokyo: Tōkyō Daigaku Shuppankai, 1966).

[†]Edited by Awaya Kentarō (Tokyo: Ōtsuki Shoten, 1987).

tions (and which Sackett kept before him during the questioning), the transcript of Kido's interrogation is far more convincing.

The questioning took place from December 1945 to March of the following year, and Sackett summoned Kido Kōichi from Sugamo Prison for over thirty full-day sessions. The transcript reveals that Sackett was a skillful interrogator. His relentless pursuit of issues relating to the emperor's use of his supreme command is especially penetrating. At times the emperor exercised this authority, on other occasions he did not. Sackett's vigorous questioning followed the course of events such as the Manchurian Incident, the Sino-Japanese war, and finally the war between Japan and the United States. In these cases, the emperor did not exercise his authority and allowed major incidents and acts of aggression. Moreover, rather than punishing those responsible for the crimes of aggression, the emperor repeatedly honored them. The names of politicians and military leaders also came up during the interrogation, and many of the people whose actions were exposed by Kido were later arrested and imprisoned or hanged. However, the transcript was not used during the Tokyo war crimes trials when it became apparent that its disclosures would implicate the emperor.

The chief prosecutor, Joseph B. Keenan, was instructed by the U.S. government not to summon the emperor to the court; he was not to be tried and punished. In accordance with the United States' national interests, attorney Sackett's interrogation of Kido was shelved.

SUPREME COMMAND AND THE EMPEROR ORGAN THEORY

Today we tend to underrate the significance of the emperor's power of supreme command in the years before and during the war, but in Japan at that time the issue was extremely important. This authority was perhaps the most unique feature of the Meiji Constitution; it was part of the sacred relationship between the military and the emperor, which neither the Diet nor the government could control.

Restrictions on the Constitutional Monarch

The prevalent view of Hirohito's role in the war absolves him of responsibility because he was a constitutional monarch and thus never decided national policy. It is argued that he accepted the decisions of the cabinet and even approved policies to which he personally was opposed. But this view is clearly in error.

In general national administrative policy the emperor, as a constitutional monarch, honored the decisions of the cabinet; he received the ministers' reports and gave his approval. Cabinet ministers were responsible for state policies—not to the people, but to the emperor. Also, the ministers were required to countersign all imperial rescripts and public ordinances. If the countersignature was missing, the rescripts and ordinances were void.

But these restrictions on imperial authority applied only to affairs of state, not to the supreme command of the military. The ministers of the army and navy, as cabinet ministers, were excluded from supreme command and thus had no control over battles, wars, military organization, and so on. The constitution gave sole authority over these matters to the emperor. Article XI of the Meiji Constitution reads: "The emperor has the supreme command of the army and navy." Article XII: "The emperor determines the organization and the peace standing of the army and navy." Article XIII: "The emperor makes war, makes peace, and concludes treaties." No constitutional provisions restricted the emperor's supreme authority. The only power the cabinet had over the military was control of the military budget. Unlike the present civilian control of the military, the cabinet then had no influence on the military's decisions about when and how to use troops.

The Meiji Constitution stipulated that only the emperor, as commander-in-chief, could control the military. The army and navy chiefs of staff were not decision-makers; they were in charge of military command under the direct authority of the emperor. The chiefs of staff essentially were intermediary agents between the emperor and the military command, and they had no final decision-making authority. With the army and navy ministers in charge only of administrative affairs, the emperor could insist that not a single soldier be moved without his permission.

Indeed, both politically and personally, the emperor cultivated a very tough image and a strict stance toward the military (almost completely opposed to the image of the deferential emperor that emerged after the war). It is said, for example, that he never allowed generals and marshals, old enough to be his father, to sit in a chair in his presence. When addressing his subjects, he dropped all honorifics. In speaking to the army chief of staff, General Sugiyama, he once said, "Say, Sugiyama, when you were war minister you said this, didn't you?" (As "you," the emperor used the term *omae,* which is a form of address used toward an "inferior.") He could exercise such boldness because he was regarded as the heir to the shining spirit of the Meiji emperor and a living god. The effect on others must have been intimidating.

By 1935, Hirohito had fifteen years of experience as the nation's ruler (including his five years as regent). He personally held the authority to appoint and dismiss cabinet ministers, generals, marshals, and other government officials and military officers, and he seemed to have no reservations about dealing with new generals. His close advisors attest that he displayed power and authority in his dealings with the military. Nevertheless, today certain conservative academics—apologists for the emperor, known in Japan as "official scholars"—are still perpetuating the widely-held myth that the emperor had very little real authority.

Tōjō Hideki and the Emperor

Even after he became prime minister, Tōjō Hideki was completely subservient in the presence of the emperor. It is said that if the emperor displayed even the slightest annoyance during a briefing with Tōjō, he immediately cut short his report and left in the middle of the audience. Some of Tōjō's close associates, including Satō Kenryō, chief of the Bureau of Military Affairs, have reported that Tōjō would appear several times at court to gauge the emperor's mood before fearfully and cautiously presenting his report.

As a result, the emperor trusted Tōjō implicitly. After the war, when Tōjō was incarcerated for war crimes in Sugamo prison, the emperor said, "No one listened to what I had to say as faithfully as Tōjō. I can't understand why people are maligning him." The emperor also said, "I don't think Tōjō was the kind of person people are saying he was. No one else carried out what I said as quickly as he."*

In the emperor's *Soliloquy*, his comments about Tōjō and his trust in his advisor stand out. The emperor apparently valued this loyal subject highly:

> Tōjō is the kind of person who, during the time he was war minister, took the decisive step of dismissing the officers who were responsible

---

*The February 12, 1946, entry of the *Sokkin Nisshi* (*Diary of an Imperial Attendant*) (Tokyo: Bungei Shunjū, 1990). This is the diary of Kinoshita Michio, the emperor's vice-chamberlain immediately after the end of the war.

for moving troops into North Indochina in defiance of the imperial command. Also, when the small fire broke out in the imperial palace, he dismissed Tanaka, the commander of the Tokyo garrison, Tajiri, the commander of the Imperial Guard Division, Brigade Commander Prince Kaya, and others. He had a solid grasp of the mind and spirit of the men in the military. When he was asked to form his cabinet I believed that as long as certain conditions were placed on him, he would keep the army under firm control and conduct state affairs smoothly.

The emperor also notes that toward the end of the war, "There were many virtuous points in Tōjō. He gave his all in carrying out his work, and whenever he spoke up it was clear that he had thought the matter over carefully."

Tōjō repeatedly asked the people to "abide by the imperial decrees with absolute fidelity." At the Tokyo war crimes trial, he caused great controversy when he testified, "As a subject, I could never make decisions that went against the emperor's wishes." This concept of loyalty is based not only on the constitutional provisions on the supreme command but also on the 1882 "Rescript to Soldiers and Sailors." (The first precept began, "The soldier and sailor should consider loyalty their essential duty.") In addition to the relationship between the emperor and the cabinet, such loyalty was an essential characteristic of the Japanese state of that time.

The Supreme Command and Responsibility for Inaction

When Prime Minister Inukai was assassinated by navy officers in the 1932 May 15th Incident, party government ended—abolished, significantly, by military terrorism. Since the establishment of party government in 1918, the head of the majority party, whose representatives in the Diet were elected freely by the people, had become the prime minister. This practice, which became common in the Taishō years, became known as Taishō democracy. After Inukai was shot, however, Admiral Saitō took over the cabinet, at the behest of the military, and the heads of the political parties no longer served as prime minister. This was a momentous turning point in Japanese political history. The parliamentary political structure that had been constitutionally established under the Taishō democratic system was destroyed through violence by the other power structure, the military. The system of constitutional monarchy, in which the emperor was expected to respect and abide by cabinet decisions, had been destroyed.

After 1932, prime ministers were appointed upon the recommendation of the elder statesman Prince Saionji, who was mindful of pressure. As a result, cabinet heads were primarily military men. The only exceptions were civilians linked to the right-wing: the bureaucrats Hirota Kōki and Konoe Fumimaro. Konoe's call for "the construction of a new world order" was similar to Hitler's, and because he was on very good terms with the army, he was pushed for the prime ministership. Though Konoe did not head a political party, he was prime minister three times. Thus, government after the assassination of Prime Minister Inukai did not represent the free will of the Japanese people. Constitutional monarchy had become an empty shell.

The emperor, however, sought to be faithful to the constitution and seemed to adhere to the "organ theory," an interpretation of the constitution that considered the state as sovereign and the emperor as an organ of the state. The organ theory offended conservatives, however, and by 1935 it was formally discarded by the Japanese government. Minobe Tatsukichi, the respected constitutional scholar and member of the House of Peers who advocated the organ theory, was forced to withdraw from public life and his publications were banned. The official interpretation of the constitution reverted to the view that the emperor held sovereignty and was not restricted by the Diet and the government. He was regarded as an absolute, sacred monarch, able to exercise transcendent authority.

Though the emperor agreed with Minobe's theory and sought to remain a constitutional monarch, the political reality was that constitutional monarchy as a ruling institution no longer existed in principle or as a system. The emperor was thus in a tragic position: the more he attempted to adhere to the principle of constitutional monarchy, the more he departed from the actual political situation and compromised his ability to lead. If the emperor had recognized the new political situation, he would have had to fulfill his responsibilities and take authority. Though the military exercised political power, the emperor could have controlled it as sovereign and commander-in-chief and on the basis of the Imperial Rescript to Soldiers and Sailors. Around 1935, the army split into two factions. The radical Kōdōha (imperial way faction) opposed democratic party government and sought to restore the emperor's power in order to extend the "imperial way" at home and abroad. The Tōseiha (control faction) also believed in strengthening military control at home and abroad, but they advocated doing so in an orderly, disciplined way to be implemented by the established military hierarchy. This split weakened the army as a political force and left it vulnerable to imperial control, which the emperor lacked the will to exert.

Though Kido Kōichi did his best to defend the emperor when he was interrogated by Henry A. Sackett prior to the Tokyo war crimes tribunal, he could not duck the question of the emperor's inaction. Kido clearly admitted the emperor's responsibility for the war and advised him to abdicate the throne.* The U.S. government, however, concluded that punishing the emperor could throw the occupation of Japan into chaos. On the basis of this political consideration, Kido's testimony was not used at the trials and the issue of Hirohito's war responsibility was avoided.

Despite the emperor's general inaction, on numerous occasions he did exercise the authority of the supreme command. In the summer of 1938, after a clash between Japanese and Soviet troops at Changgufeng, on the border of Manchuria and Soviet Siberia, the army decided to take military action against the Soviet Union. War Minister Itagaki Seishirō and Chief of Staff Prince Kan'in went to the imperial court to get the emperor's approval for the action, but the emperor refused to sanction military action. He said:

> In truth, the army's behavior is outrageous. In the Manchurian incident . . . and the Marco Polo Bridge incident, the forces overseas acted arbitrarily, refusing to obey orders from central headquarters. The army frequently employs base methods that are totally unworthy of my army. . . . Henceforth not a single one of my troops is to be moved without my command.[†]

The forces at the front, however, refused to follow the emperor's command and launched a night attack on the Soviet troops. The successful Soviet counterattack left 1,440 Japanese dead or wounded. But again, as in the Manchurian Incident, the emperor failed to punish those responsible.

The emperor forcefully expressed his will in many other areas as well, not just war strategy and the deployment of troops. When the Japan-Germany-Italy tripartite alliance was being negotiated, the important concern for Japan was whether or not it would be required to support Germany and Italy in case of war. The Japanese ambassadors to Germany and Italy, following the wishes of the army but without obtaining the

---

Kido Kōichi Nikki, October 17, 1951, entry.

[†]Harada Kumao, *Saionji-kō to Seikyoku (Prince Saionji and the Political Situation)*, 9 vols., July 11, 1938 entry (Tokyo: Iwanami Shoten, 1950–1956).

emperor's approval, informed their host governments that Japan would join a war on behalf of either side. Hearing this news, the emperor asked War Minister Itagaki, "By indicating that Japan will join them in war without my knowledge does this not mean that the two ambassadors have violated the supreme imperial authority?" and "In general the supreme authority to declare war and conclude peace is under my jurisdiction. It is therefore unconscionable that people should make any demands without my permission or without even speaking to me."*

These words make it quite clear that the emperor was more than just a state organ who "reigns but does not rule" or, as some of the "official scholars" would have it, an automaton who only rubber-stamped the policies already decided upon by the cabinet.

Directing the Makeup of the Cabinet

The August 28 entry of Prince Saionji's diary mentions the emperor's active attempts to influence the formation of a new cabinet:

> The emperor, in an unprecedented move, designated Umezu Yoshijirō and Hata Shunroku as candidates for the position of war minister. . . . The emperor then questioned the prime minister about cabinet ministers with whom he was concerned. [He said,] "Do your best to get Umezu or Hata. Even if the three chiefs of the army offices make a decision and come to me, I have no intention of accepting their advice. Now, run the government in accordance with the constitution. I believe it is to Japan's advantage to make use of England and America in foreign affairs, and this being the kind of time it is, I have a special interest in the selection of cabinet ministers for the home ministry, ministry of justice, foreign ministry, and finance ministry."†

These points are verified by the emperor's *Soliloquy:*

> In the formation of the Abe Cabinet, the most important issue was the selection of the war minister. At that time the newspapers were mentioning as candidates for that post Lt. General Isogai [Rensuke] and another officer, but if these two were picked there would be a danger of a

*Ibid., April 10, 1939, entry.

†Ibid., August 28, 1939, 1939, entry.

revival of the moves to conclude a Japan-German alliance. So I ordered Abe to appoint either Umezu or Hata war minister.

The emperor thus was actively involved in the crucial affairs of state; he certainly was not the passive constitutional monarch that the official scholars (and Hirohito himself, in postwar years) have so convincingly portrayed. The emperor's true role is becoming clearer as many documents, including the diaries of the emperor's close advisers, come to light. Some documents were hidden to protect the emperor at the time of the Tokyo war crimes trials, but about ten years after the trials, documents began to surface, some hidden in metal cans buried in backyards or left in rural areas where evacuees from the cities went during the war. It is very likely many more important materials remain undisclosed today.

THE DECLARATION OF WAR AGAINST AMERICA AND ENGLAND

At the outbreak of the Second World War, powerful groups in the army, the bureaucracy, and the political parties agitated for aggression on the continent. Nonetheless, a small number of officials among the emperor's close attendants still favored good relations with England and the United States. In the Foreign Ministry, officials like Shidehara Kijūrō and Yoshida Shigeru and, in the military, some like naval leader Yonai Mitsumasa, urged caution.

The Japanese financial-business sector also did not unanimously favor war. Though the newly risen *zaibatsu*—companies like Shōwa Electric, Japan Nitrogen Fertilizer (later Chisso), Riken, and Nissan—cooperated with the military's call for a new world order, the older firms, by and large, wanted to preserve and protect the interests in hand. They were reluctant to risk engaging in dangerous new military ventures.

Between the years 1930 and 1941, these various power groups and interests engaged in a tug of war, hidden from the eyes of the people. The mass media supported the hard-line military faction and guided public opinion toward war. I believe that the emperor sided with his more cautious advisors but was swept along by the rapidly changing tide of events.

The final decision to go to war with the United States and England was made at the imperial conference of December 1, 1941. (The combined fleet assigned to attack Hawaii had left the Kurile Islands off Hokkaidō five days before.) The unanimous decision of the Tōjō cabinet, the army, and navy was made official with the emperor's approval. If the emperor had insisted on caution, the decision for war might have been postponed, but it was impossible to reverse the decision for war at this late stage. Undoubtedly the emperor's reasoning was complex.

His sentiments were revealed vividly in the *Soliloquy*. The entries covering the period from the formation of the Tōjō cabinet in October of 1941 to December 1, when the decision for war was formally made, reveal the emperor's personal thoughts for the first time. When the emperor ordered Tōjō to form a new cabinet, he told him to scrap the decision, made on September 6, to plan for war and to "do your best to achieve a peaceful solution."

> Tōjō . . . sought to void the decision made at the imperial conference of September 6th and held liaison conferences daily for a week without sleeping, but the key issues could not be resolved.
>
> [Navy war councilor, Admiral] Oikawa's plan to avoid war was to produce synthetic oil in Japan. But to do so, two million tons of iron would have been needed—supplied by the army and navy. Also, a large number of factories would have had to be used to produce the oil, bringing domestic industrial production to a virtual standstill. If this policy had been followed Japan would have been defeated without going to war.
>
> The oil embargo really drove Japan up against the wall. The prevailing opinion, that it would be better to try to win even if it meant we had to count on some unexpected good luck, was natural in that situation. If I had gone against the advocates of war, the public would no doubt have thought that we were meekly surrendering to America when our army and navy had superior forces, and a coup d'etat would have been staged. It was truly a trying time. Then the ultimatum from Secretary Hull arrived: in the realm of diplomacy also we had come to a dead end.

Negotiations between the United States and Japan had been underway since March 1941, but the two countries' political and economic differences could not be resolved. Finally, on November 27, Secretary of State Cordell Hull submitted to the Japanese envoys the same proposal that had been presented at the beginning of the negotiations. Because this terse note signified that the months of negotiation had been for nothing, Tōjō and the army officials regarded it as a de facto ultimatum. Final preparations for war began.

The emperor had hoped to use an imperial conference with cabinet ministers and senior statesmen to prevent war, but the advocates of peace—Konoe Fumimaro, Hiranuma Kiichirō, Yonai Mitsumasa, Okada Keisuke, Hirota Kōki, Abé Nobuyuki, and Hayashi Senjūrō—did not speak forcefully enough to save Japan from the disaster of war. These officials, too, bear some responsibility for the outbreak of war.

The next day, Prince Takamatsu came to see his older brother, the emperor. The exchange of opinions on this occasion is important. At this decisive moment, the emperor was still citing technicalities to justify his decision to fight. He gave no thought to the people, who would suffer the most:

> Prince Takamatsu came to inquire about yesterday's meeting. He expressed the view that, "If we miss this opportunity [to continue negotiations with the United States and resolve the differences], we will not be able to avoid war. From December 1 the navy will move to a war footing. Once that happens it will be impossible to stop them." We also discussed the possible outcome of the war. According to the prince, the Supreme War Council estimated the chances for victory to be fifty-fifty, and sixty-forty if things went well. I told him that I thought we might lose. The prince then said that if that was the case I should put a stop to it then. I held the view that being a monarch of a constitutional state, I had to approve the unanimous opinion of the government and the Supreme War Council. If I failed to do so, Tōjō would resign and there would be a major coup d'état, and the completely reckless advocates of war would gain control.
>
> On December 1 the combined meeting of cabinet ministers and War Council members was held at the imperial conference, and the decision for war was made. I did not say a word on that occasion because I believed that it would have been futile to oppose the war.

Kojima Noburu, author of the massive work *Tennō* [*Emperor*],* remarked upon reading this section of the *Soliloquy:*

> I wonder about his explanation that he agreed with the decision to go to war because he was afraid that a coup d'état or a civil war would break out. . . . I feel like asking him which is better: the outbreak of a coup d'état or the road to defeat and destruction of the nation.†

*5 vols. (Tokyo: Bungei Shunjū, 1974).

†Kojima Noburu, "Examining the *Soliloquy,*" *Bungei Shunjū,* January 1991.

It is astonishing that the emperor, whose royal authority had the absolute support of the Japanese people and whose supreme power was based on the constitution, would say that he thought his opposition futile and so remained silent at the decisive moment. At that time, civil war was almost impossible and the imperial system was sustained in a well-ordered fashion. Was the emperor actually so afraid of a group of army officers? Did he not consider relying on the support of the many in the armed forces and the vast number among the public who were willing to die for him? If he really opposed the war, why didn't he try to prevent it, even if it meant risking his life, in order to save many more lives?

> Whatever may happen to me
> I put a stop to the war
> Thinking only of the people who are dying

Those who died in the war would surely regret that the emperor did not write this poem before, rather than after, the war.

The Emperor's Shifting Mood

Once the war started, Japanese forces achieved unexpected victories in the sea battles of Hawaii and the coast of Malaya and in the fall of Singapore. The emperor's mood changed completely with these successes. Kido Kōichi recorded in his diary that the emperor's "royal face was especially radiant, and he was smiling. He remarked, 'We are winning so many victories so quickly.'"

With each report of victory, the people rejoiced wildly and shouted, "*Tennō Heika banzai!*" (Long live his imperial majesty!) In response, the emperor approved new military operations and inspired and encouraged his officers, soldiers, and sailors. The war guidance staff members of the Imperial Headquarters were deeply moved by the emperor's actions. One member wrote in the journal, "His Glorious Majesty, the sanctity of the supreme authority is boundless. I realize the falsity of the emperor organ theory for the first time in serving in this war. Ah!"*

Thus the emperor impressed his staff and shrewdly reaped the benefits of his "personal decisions." But in 1943, after the United States launched

*Daihonei Kimitsu Sensō Nisshi (Secret War Journal of the Imperial Headquarters), entry for March 13, 1942.

an all-out offensive and the tide of the war shifted, the emperor's anxiety began to increase. He pressed the chief of staff:

> If we continue fighting in this manner, it will be like Guadalcanal. It will only raise the fighting spirit of the enemy, and then the neutral countries will start to waver, China will get big-headed, and the impact on the countries in the Greater East Asian Co-Prosperity Sphere will be enormous. Can't you somehow beat down the American forces head on at some front?
>
> All the battle fronts look bad. Can't you give the American forces a walloping?
>
> If we continue to get pushed back steadily this way, it will have a significant impact on other countries, not just on the enemy. Now, just where are you going to show some success? Where are you going to stage a decisive battle?*

No doubt these words were conveyed to the staff officers directing the war effort and prompted desperate attacks and huge sacrifices. In the Pacific islands, suicide attacks were launched continuously. It appears that the emperor was constantly thinking of ways to end the war favorably by inflicting a crushing blow on the U.S. forces at some front.

A Crushing Blow

The *Soliloquy* shows many examples of the emperor's hope that Japan could achieve a stinging victory in the Leyte campaign, the battle of Okinawa, and the Burma campaign. He reveals a great interest in the strategy of these operations:

> The best policy would have been . . . to defend the Philippines. I disagreed with the army and navy general staffs, and believed that we should have struck hard at Leyte. Then, with America staggering, we would have been able to find room for a compromise. But my opinion did not reach the Supreme War Council. The army, navy and Yamashita all disagreed. For this reason Yamashita failed to make vigorous use of the troops; he was fighting reluctantly. And the navy recklessly sent out the fleet, engaged in battle in an unscientific fashion, and failed.
>
> Navy Chief of Staff Oikawa was still firmly confident of victory in a decisive battle in Okinawa, despite the defeat in the battle of the

---

*Sugiyama Memo, 2 vols. (Tokyo: Hara Shobsō, 1967), entry for August 5, 1943.

Philippines. I had lost any hope for victory after the enemy forces broke through the Stanley forests in New Guinea [September, 1943]. I wanted to grasp the chance to quickly conclude a negotiated peace after striking a crushing blow on the enemy someplace. But we had an agreement with Germany not to conclude a peace settlement unilaterally, so from the standpoint of international good faith I did not want to negotiate ahead of them. For that reason I even hoped for a quick German defeat.

After the defeat at Okinawa there was no hope for a sea battle. I decided the only hope was to strike at Yunnan, coordinating it with the Burma campaign. Then this would inflict a considerable blow to England and America. When I mentioned this to Umezu, he opposed it, saying that we could not continue to send supplies there.

It is surprising not only how well versed the emperor was in military operations but also how rationally he analyzed the situations in Leyte and Okinawa. Even after total defeat in the battle of Okinawa, he did not abandon hope and instead spoke of striking at Yunnan Province in China. Here we see the profile of a "fighting emperor."

The situation became even more hopeless after the Japanese navy suffered a major defeat at the sea battle off the Mariana islands. Saipan and Guam were occupied by the United States and were used as a base for launching massive air raids on Japan itself. Beginning with Tokyo, all the major cities were subjected to air attacks and burned. Endangered children were evacuated to the rural communities, and those remaining behind were conscripted into labor and suffered conditions akin to those on the battlefields. Most people believed in the emperor and were committed to dedicating their lives to the nation, at great sacrifice.

However, in June and July of 1944, following the fall of Saipan, the war leadership staff saw the writing on the wall:

We can no longer direct the war with any hope of success. The only course left is for Japan's one hundred million people to sacrifice their lives by charging the enemy to make them lose the will to fight.

In judging the situation . . . there is unanimous agreement that henceforth we will slowly fall into a state of ruin. So it is necessary to plan for a quick end to the war.*

If at this point the emperor had made a desperate effort, even if it meant sacrificing his own life, many others would have been spared.

---

*The Secret War Journal of the Imperial Headquarters, June 24 and July 1, 1944 entries.

The "Sacred Decision" to End the War

Certainly, the emperor's decision to accept the Potsdam Declaration in August 1945 helped avoid the tragedy of the decisive battle in Japan itself, planned by the U.S. armed forces. Admirers of the emperor treat this "noble decision" as if it were a blessing from the gods. But what excuse can be made for the needless suffering and death of millions of innocent victims in Japan and its neighboring nations in Asia?

I do not believe, as David Bergamini states in his book *Japan's Imperial Conspiracy*, that the emperor prolonged the war to satisfy his love of war or his malicious intentions.* Emperor Hirohito was a complex person. He was not like the Meiji emperor, who possessed a heroic spirit and was very decisive. Hirohito castigated but did not punish the militarists for their arbitrary actions and, as a result, some of the top military officials did not take him seriously. In the end, the emperor was dragged along by the military. He exercised his sovereign authority only after the Potsdam Declaration had been issued, the atomic bombs had been dropped on Hiroshima and Nagasaki, and the Soviet forces had launched their attack. The situation had become so desperate that no other way out was available. The emperor finally made his "sacred decision" when he was asked to do so by Prime Minister Suzuki Kantarō.

Before dawn on August 14, 1945, the last imperial conference was held in the underground air raid shelter of the imperial palace. There the emperor declared his intention to accept the terms of the Potsdam Declaration. Konoe Fumimaro heard what had transpired at that conference and told his secretary, Hosokawa Morisada, about it. Konoe's account is recorded in the August 14 entry of the *Hosokawa Diary*:

> His Majesty summoned the cabinet ministers and spoke out forcefully: "I do not care about what may happen to me. I cannot continue the war any longer, for I cannot bear to see the suffering of the people." All the ministers in the room cried out at hearing these words. Subsequently, it was decided to make public the text accepting the terms of the Potsdam Declaration.†

*David Bergamini, *Japan's Imperial Conspiracy: How Emperor Hirohito Led Japan into War against the West*. New York: Morrow, 1971.

†Hosokawa Morisada, *Hosokawa Nikki (Hosokawa Diary)*, 2 vols. (Tokyo: Chūō Bunko, 1989).

A similar account is given in *Shūsen-hishi* *(The Secret History of the End of the War)* by Shimomura Kainan, then chief of the Information Bureau.* Although the reference to the suffering of the people probably occurred, the detailed description in the *Shūsen-hishi* shows that the final two meetings of the imperial conference were not most urgently concerned with saving people's lives. Rather, the conference dealt mainly with how to defend the *kokutai,* the so-called national essence or national polity—that is, the emperor system.

Kinoshita's *Diary and the Emperor's* Soliloquy

The most valuable source on the emperor's actions immediately after the war is the earlier-mentioned *Sokkin Nisshi* *(Diary of an Imperial Attendant)* by Kinoshita Michio, deputy grand chamberlain. Kinoshita served as a close attendant of the emperor during the difficult period from just before the end of the war until the end of May 1946. His diary details not only activities within the imperial court but also the emperor's version of the course of the war. As the Tokyo war crimes trials neared, Kido Kōichi and many senior statesmen, including the emperor's uncle, Prince Nashimoto, were taken to Sugamo prison beginning in December 1945. Kinoshita undoubtedly felt it necessary to prepare for the possibility that the emperor, too, might have to face the tribunal. He and five other imperial attendants thus sought to ascertain the true history of the war from the emperor. Of course, Kinoshita was completely loyal to the emperor and so endeavored to defend him.

In addition to Kinoshita's diary, the emperor's *Soliloquy* records the same material, transcribed by another of the five attendants, Terasaki Hidenari. Terasaki was chief secretary at the Japanese embassy in Washington when the Pacific War broke out. Shortly after, he returned to Japan with his American wife Gwendolyn and their daughter Mariko. He served as an information officer and liaison between the imperial court and the Japanese government and the U.S. GHQ authorities when the war ended. He became an official attendant of the emperor, had close relations with GHQ's Brigadier General Fellers, a relative of his wife, and was made chief of the Information Bureau of the Foreign Ministry and an intermediary between the emperor and MacArthur.

*Shimomura Kainan, *Shūsen-hishi* (Tokyo: Kōdansha, 1950).

On October 16, 1946, he accompanied the emperor on a visit to MacArthur at the U.S. embassy and "reverently recorded" the meeting. If Terasaki had remained alive, confidential information about this period would have been available, but he died of illness in 1951 at the young age of fifty. Following his death, his wife and daughter returned to America.

Years later, at the home of his daughter Mariko Terasaki Miller, 170 pages of Terasaki stationery were found that contained the transcription of the emperor's *Soliloquy*. The find was made public in the fall of 1990, after the enthronement ceremony of Emperor Akihito. At the beginning of the account, the following introduction was added by Terasaki:

> This is a record of the recollections of His Majesty resulting from a total of five meetings extending over a total time span of over eight hours. His Majesty related to the five court officials, Lord Privy Seal Matsudaira [Keimin], Deputy Grand Chamberlian Kinoshita (Grand Chamberlain Fujita was ill and resting), Chief of Imperial Household Affairs Matsudaira [Yasumasa], Internal Record Section Chief Inada and Court Attendant Terasaki his recollections about the indirect and direct causes of the Greater East Asian War, the course of events and the circumstances at the time of the termination of the war. His Majesty did not refer to any memos at the meetings.
>
> During the first three meetings, His Majesty had a slight cold and so was resting in his library. He had a bed delivered to the room where he dealt with political affairs, and resting on this temporary bed, he spoke to us. The last two meetings were held at Hayama imperial villa where he was resting. The five of us went to Hayama and listened to his account. The transcription was made mainly by Inada. When some points needed clarification Kinoshita asked His Majesty about them and made amendations.
>
> June 1, 1946

When the emperor began his discussion on March 18, 1946, the United States already had decided not to try him as a war criminal. But at that time it was not clear what demands might be made of him by the governments of China, the Soviet Union, or Australia. The following is from his conclusion:

> At the outbreak of the war I approved the decision of the Tōjō cabinet because, as a constitutional monarch under a constitutional government, I had no alternative but to do so. If I approved what I favored and disapproved what I was against, then I would have been no different than an absolute monarch.

At the time of the war's end, the situation was different. Since government officials could not agree, Prime Minister Suzuki asked me to make the decision. Therefore, I acted on the basis of what I believed was right for the good of the nation and the people.

As I think back on the situation, I believe my thinking in the first case was correct. Considering the fact that something like a coup d'état was attempted at the end of the war in protest of the unconditional surrender when the military power of the army and navy had been exhuasted, think of what would have happened if I had vetoed the cabinet's decision for war.

If I had not permitted the armed forces, which had first-rate men who had undergone years of training, to spring into action, then as time passed the supply of oil would have been depleted and the fleet would have been unable to move. If we had turned to the production of synthetic oil to supply our needs, it would have required virtually all of our industrial capacity. The nation would then have fallen into ruin, and if the other powers had made demands on Japan, Japan would have perished: in those circumstances we would have been presented with impossible conditions by the other powers, and we would have had to surrender unconditionally.

This was the prospect facing Japan at the time of the outbreak of the war. If I had vetoed the decision for war at the time, a huge internal rebellion would have broken out. The people whom I relied on in my circle would have been killed, and my own life would have been endangered. That does not matter, but a brutal, ferocious war would have ensued, and tragedies several times greater than what took place in the current war would have occurred. A situation would have arisen wherein the end of the war could not be negotiated, and Japan would have been destroyed, I believe.

Is Emperor Hirohito's historical perception correct? Many important questions were not addressed in the conclusion of the *Soliloquy*. Would the emperor's justification of his actions on the basis of his role as constitutional monarch be valid under the circumstances noted in these conclusions? And what about his rationale that he decided on a war that he disapproved of because he feared a hypothetical coup d'état?

The Magnanimous Spirit of Emperor Hirohito

> *Whatever may happen to me*
> *I put a stop to the war*
> *Thinking only of the people who were dying*

This well-known poem was broadcast repeatedly over the airwaves on the day of Emperor Hirohito's funeral, and it revived the popular belief that he was Japan's great savior for having made the "sacred decision" at the risk of his own life. This point was emphasized repeatedly, but if one looks at where and how this poem first appeared, the story becomes more complex.

The poem, along with three others, was entered in the Kinoshita diary on December 15, 1945, under the title, *Thoughts at the End of the War.* "After seeing the poems," Kinoshita wrote, "I asked His Majesty if I could receive His Majesty's permission to make the poems public, making sure that they would not be used for propagandistic ends." Until then, emperors' poems were seldom made public. Of the four poems, the following reflects reality at the end of the war most accurately:

> *Wishing to preserve the national essence*
> *I ended the war*
> *Though I may have to walk a path of thorns*

The heart of this poem indicates Hirohito's desire to preserve the *koku-tai*, the national polity or essence that centered upon the emperor, no matter how thorny the path turned out to be. The next poem reads:

> *Thinking of the people dying endlessly in the air raids*
> *I ended the war*
> *Having no thought of my own fate*

Hirohito recently had received news of the atomic bombings of Hiroshima and Nagasaki, and under these circumstances he decided that war could no longer be prolonged.

But only one poem was publicized, made famous in order to stress the emperor's magnanimous spirit. This image and the one in MacArthur's *Reminiscences* have become the mythology of the end of the war. The person who had been regarded as a god came before the general and begged, "I come to see you, General MacArthur, to offer myself to the judgment of the powers you represent as the one to bear sole responsibility for every political and military decision made and action taken by my people in the conduct of the war."*

---

*Douglas MacArthur, *Reminiscences* (New York: McGraw-Hill, 1964), p. 288.

Not only did people sympathize with the emperor's sentiments, dire rumors began to spread: the emperor was ill, the emperor had committed suicide, the emperor would abdicate. This folklore that accompanied the war defeat helped to sustain the emperor system during a period of chaos. Gentle criticism of the emperor also consolidated the public perception that the emperor was free of responsibility. History is often made and buttressed by myths and folklore rather than facts. Conscious of this fact, the emperor's close attendants wrote and publicized things that would foster such myths and folklore.

The Question of Abdication

An interesting item in the diary of Yabe Teiji (1902–1967) concerns a discussion of the emperor's possible abdication. Yabe was a professor of law of Tokyo Imperial University who served in the Navy Ministry, Foreign Ministry, and Greater East Asia Ministry. He was a consultant for the cabinet and cooperated fully with the war effort. In the 1950s, because of his ties with Prime Minister Nakasone Yasuhiro, he was appointed president of Takushoku University.

On January 14, 1946, Yabe, who had just resigned his professorship, was invited to the home of his friend Prince Takamatsu. He was received informally and asked about "democracy and the emperor system." The discussion between the prince and Yabe reveals the sense of insecurity—also evident in Kinoshita's account—that prevailed at the imperial court.

Prince Takamatsu told Yabe that if the emperor were to abdicate, "some people say that he would be prosecuted as a war criminal." Yabe noted, "I told him that if they are going to pursue this matter, they will do so whether the emperor has abdicated or not."

Clearly Prince Takamatsu was worried not only that the emperor would take responsibility for the war by abdicating but also that the emperor would be prosecuted as a war criminal. Yabe seems to have believed that the best way to preserve the emperor system was to deflect the pressure from the occupation authorities by having the emperor abdicate and democratizing the imperial court. Toward the end of the entry, he wrote:

> The prince said that if we say that the emperor system is good for Japan, the other side might target this institution all the more. I said that I think this will be the case, and for that reason we must democ-

ratize it as much as possible. Then we can only make use of the people's will, as defined in the Potsdam Declaration, as a shield.

Yabe's democratization did not conflict with the emperor system: it was a democratization with limits. Yabe's view represents the thinking of the rulers and official scholars at that time, when the future of the emperor and the emperor system was most precarious. They proposed using the people's support for the emperor "as a shield" against the external forces threatening the emperor system. Their strategy was, first (in the words of the then-popular slogan), expressions of "one hundred million people repenting together." Secondly, they had the emperor visit MacArthur often, swear to abide by the Potsdam Declaration, and venture out among the people to win their support. Democratization was started in this fashion and was completed with the wedding of Crown Prince Akihito, who overturned the tradition of marrying within the royal circle by choosing the daughter of a businessman as his wife.

THE OCCUPATION

Sacrificing Okinawa

In the mid-seventies, Shindō Eiichi, professor of international relations at Tsukuba University, discovered two important unpublished documents in the National Archives in Washington: a September 20, 1947, memo to MacArthur from William J. Sebald, diplomatic section chief of GHQ and later U.S. ambassador to Japan; and a September 22, 1947, memo from Sebald to George C. Marshall, then the secretary of state. These two memos relay a message from the emperor brought to Sebald in mid-September by Terasaki Hidenari, chief of the Imperial Household Agency:

> According to Terasaki, the emperor hopes that the United States will continue its military occupation of Okinawa and the Ryukyu Islands. In the emperor's opinion this will be beneficial to the United States and it also will ensure Japan's defense. The people of Japan fear the threat from Russia, and its intervention in Japan's domestic political affairs. So this policy will have broad support. . . . According to the emperor, the military occupation of Okinawa should be instituted under the legal fiction that a long-term lease (25 to 50 years) has been extended to the United States by Japan, which retains its sovereignty over the islands.

The memo also notes that the negotiations should be conducted by Japan and the United States in secret. This message from the emperor was welcomed by George Kennan, chief of the Policy Planning Division of the State Department, who was concerned with containment of the Soviet Union as well as with formulating a peace treaty with Japan. Kennan emphasized the importance of a long-term occupation of Okinawa to the U.S. government and urged that the emperor's message be used in deciding U.S. policy on this question.

Of course, this proposal was not conceived by the emperor himself. High government officials in the Katayama cabinet advocated turning Okinawa into a U.S. military base for the defense of Japan. But this message undeniably was sent by the emperor, as clearly stated in grand chamberlain Iriye Sukemasa's diary, which recently has been made public.

The Okinawa proposal was made while the Tokyo war crimes trials were in progress. Around that time, prosecuting attorney Joseph Keenan and Tōjō were engaged in a heated exchange concerning the emperor's responsibility. (Keenan became agitated when Tōjō testified that only the emperor had the authority to decide to go to war with the United States and England.)

Why was the emperor's message delivered to GHQ at this particular time? The influence of the international situation—with the Cold War between the United States and the Soviet Union beginning and the Tokyo trials underway—cannot be ignored. The emperor's message was delivered before the United States had asked to convert Okinawa into a long-term base. Though the Potsdam Declaration had pledged to Japan that the occupation forces would be withdrawn once peace was restored and a democratic government had been established, the emperor voluntarily offered Okinawa to the United States.

When Professor Shindō revealed this information in detail in the October 1979 issue of the magazine *Sekai,* the people of Okinawa were understandably shocked. (Amazingly, though, intellectuals, the mass media, and the general public in Japan proper remained relatively indifferent to this revelation.) The Battle of Okinawa at the end of the war was designed to protect the emperor and the Japanese main islands. To this end, close to 100,000 soldiers died in battle and nearly 200,000 Okinawans lost their lives. What followed was a long period of direct control by the U.S. forces, a military occupation that cut off Okinawa from the rest of Japan. The people of Okinawa believed that when the peace treaty was signed they would be reunited with Japan. But without their knowledge, four years prior to the signing of the peace treaty, the emperor they believed to be benevolent had offered Okinawa to the United States.

The emperor's message reflects fear of the influence of the Soviet Union and communism. This fear was intensified because, at the time the emperor's message was delivered to Sebald, the Japan Communist Party had gained a great deal of strength and labor and peasant movements were rapidly swinging to the left. The emperor must have realized the serious threat that these ideologies posed to the existing institutions. As Sebald concluded, the emperor's offer held an ulterior motive. "It smells of egoism," he noted in his comments.

The year 1947 was a time of extreme uncertainty and anxiety for Japan's rulers because it was not clear what turn the Tokyo trials might suddenly take. Ten days after the emperor's message was delivered, Chief Prosecutor Keenan issued this pronouncement: "The emperor will not be called before the court for any reason whatever. He will not be subpoenaed, even as a witness."

The National Tours

Toward the end of the war, the emperor was in an extremely difficult position, but he displayed unique talent as a leader. He controlled the inflexible factions in the military leadership, prevented a third atomic bomb from being dropped on Japan, averted a decisive battle in Japan itself, and ended the war. He then labored desperately to ease U.S. occupation policy.

To accomplish the last objective, the emperor emerged from the isolation of the imperial palace to stand before the people. For five years beginning in February 1946, he made exhaustive tours of the country. During his journeys, he reached out to the public and emotionally aroused a people who had lost their spiritual mooring. He went to every corner of the land—to isolated fishing and mountain villages, mines, factories, and schools. He visited those wounded in the war, families of soldiers who had died in the war, hospitals, and so on. He called out to the people, consoling and encouraging the sick and weary. He carried out this ambitious project with missionary zeal. Even enlightened statesmen could not have matched this performance. His activities during this period are a testament to the unique qualities Emperor Hirohito possessed as a national leader.

The idea for the tour did not originate with the emperor or his close advisers; it was the suggestion of Colonel Kenneth Dyke, chief of the Civil Information and Education Section of GHQ. Dyke was reacting to the threat of famine that loomed over Japan. Imperial aide Kinoshita summarized Dyke's memo in his diary entry of January 13, 1946:

> The emperor must go beyond simply issuing royal edicts to make his views public. He must get in touch with the people personally and arouse and foster the people's pride and patriotism by demonstrating a sincerity that is consistent in word and action.
>
> Driven by strong self-interest to make money, in Japan proper black market transactions and black market centers are flourishing. This demonstrates the decline in the moral character of the Japanese. In order to correct this situation and make equitable distribution of food, thus eliminating the need for black markets, the conscience of the Japanese must be awakened and aroused. This cannot be accomplished by the force of military administration. Only the emperor can accomplish this. I believe this may be the best opportunity. The emperor should tour the country extensively, visit the mines and the farm villages, and listen to what the people have to say. He should converse with them, ask them all sorts of questions, and listen to their ideas. After the end of his tour he should address all the people by calling upon them to demonstrate a spirit of self-sacrifice, arouse their sense of responsibility as a people, and their aspirations for the future of their race, and awaken their conscience.
>
> For instance, he could say to them, "People of Japan, there is a food shortage in Japan today. People without food are getting thinner day by day. Why don't those of us who have surplus food show the same spirit of sacrifice that we demonstrated during the war and distribute food to our fellow countrymen, to every corner of the land? By doing so we will be able to fulfill our responsibility to our nation and to the international community.
>
> "Today we as a people may appear to be in decline, but basically we possess a powerful latent energy. We have the potential to make unparalleled contributions to world culture, especially in literature, religion and the people's way of life."
>
> The emperor should exhort the people by speaking to them in this manner.

Kinoshita goes on to note that "the emperor enthusiastically agreed with the suggestion." Though Emperor Hirohito deserves credit for this act of atonement, the people of Japan were not told that the emperor's tour was undertaken on the recommendation of the occupation authorities, who used him to facilitate their governing of Japan.

The emperor's tours of Japan required him to display a great deal of courage and to endure considerable hardship. He covered all corners of Japan (except Okinawa)—twenty-two prefectures in all, about half of the prefectures in the country. He slept in the train he was traveling on, stayed in simple inns, and personally visited families whose members had died in battle or of sickness at the front. He visited hospital patients and those who had been repatriated from abroad. He called out to and spoke with a large number of people. He even patted children's heads. His activities were unprecedented, and the people's reaction was frenzied. Many undoubtedly were amazed that a person who had so recently been looked upon as a divine being would undertake such activities.

Japanese public opinion toward the emperor in those years was certainly in his favor. Toward the end of the war, Nosaka Sanzō, later the chairman of the Japan Communist Party, conducted a survey among several hundred Japanese POWs in Yenan, China. He asked their views about their leaders, including the emperor. According to this survey, known as the "Nosaka Notes," only 31 percent of the POWs had confidence in their commanding officers, but almost 99 percent of the soldiers revered the emperor absolutely. This survey was conducted soon after the soldiers had been captured by the communist Chinese Eighth Route Army, before any attempts had been made to indoctrinate them with communist ideology. Nosaka concluded, probably correctly, that most Japanese soldiers held similar views and that ordinary Japanese also felt this way. These observations led Nosaka, upon his return to Japan, to advocate a soft line toward the emperor and a united, popular front with other left-wing groups. However, upon their release from Japanese prisons, many leftist leaders who had been persecuted under the Peace Preservation Law took over the executive committee of the Japan Communist Party and overruled Nosaka, and the popular front failed to materialize.

The observations of some of Japan's prominent liberal thinkers are also an interesting window on contemporary views of the emperor's war guilt. Nakano Yoshio, a tough-minded scholar of English literature, wrote an essay entitled "A Confession," in which he argued for the abolition of the emperor system, but he carefully explained that this suggestion was completely unrelated to his personal feelings about the emperor:

> I am an ordinary citizen who has absolutely no ties to the emperor, but I do not know of any other Japanese toward whom I feel the kind of profound sense of respect and affection as I feel toward Emperor Hirohito. I have absolutely no taste for criticizing the emperor with a

shower of vulgar personal insults, vilification or ridicule. I believe the emperor system must be abolished, but the emperor as a person is another matter.

In June 1946, the poet Miyoshi Tatsuji also confessed to similar sentiments. He said that he respected the emperor but "as the supreme leader of the nation, he must on his own initiative assume primary responsibility for defeat in this war."

One might have expected the people to hold the emperor accountable for the defeat in the war and to view him with hatred or resentment. But instead, somewhat miraculously, the people's admiration for the emperor surged again after his national tours.

But the rekindling of affection between the emperor and the people had a powerful effect on the Tokyo trials, and in 1948 GHQ asked the emperor to restrain his activities. The Soviet Union, China, and Australia argued that the emperor was deliberately attempting to intimidate the War Crimes Tribunal by stirring up the people's frenzied enthusiasm. The tours were thus canceled and, for the time being, the emperor remained quietly in Tokyo.

On December 23, 1948, the date of the present emperor's birthday (Akihito, then the crown prince), seven of the class-A war criminals who had been judged guilty by the International Military Tribunal for the Far East were hanged.

December 23, 1948, also marks the beginning of the second phase of the emperor's travels. In 1949 and 1950, he visited all of the prefectures in the southern islands of Kyūshū and Shikoku. Thus, by the time the San Francisco Peace Treaty was signed in 1951, the emperor had traveled to almost all of the prefectures in Japan. (He went to the northern island of Hokkaidō by plane in 1954.) Strictly speaking, from 1946 to 1951, when the Japanese government regained its sovereignty by signing the peace treaty, the emperor journeyed throughout Japan to establish a close relationship with the people.

The details of the emperor's travels were recorded in Grand Chamberlain Iriye Sukemasa's diary, and a record was issued by every prefecture called "The Journal of the Royal Tours." The journals are oral accounts by those who were spoken to by the emperor, who were offered the emperor's best wishes and condolences, and so on. These accounts give the impression that the people's affection and respect for the emperor increased over the prewar years. Of course, some people sneered at the apparent hypocrisy of the tour, but virtually everyone accepted the emperor's concerns and feelings at face value. The historical records portray gentle, innocent citizens who quickly forget the past.*

The imperial tours of the outlying regions served U.S. interests by aiding the implementation of GHQ's occupation policies. The tours took place as strikes were spreading throughout the country and in all sectors of industry. At the same time, left-wing forces were rapidly gaining strength. The United States saw the public's affection and respect for the emperor as a positive force to counter these developments. This strategy is revealed clearly in Colonel Kenneth Dyke's suggestion, mentioned earlier, and in the third "Record of the Imperial Interview," in which Emperor Hirohito told MacArthur that "strikes are what will hinder" postwar recovery. The emperor said that he regretted that

> the level of education of the Japanese is still low, and their religious faith is still weak. There are many people who, seeing strikes being staged in America, conclude that by staging strikes Japan, too, can become a democratic nation. Moreover, there are third party elements who seek to further their own interests by taking advantage of the poor conditions of the country. The future of national economic recovery is truly worrisome.

General MacArthur replied, "I agree. The communists are attempting to gain power by making all sorts of verbal promises to the uneducated." He consoled the emperor, however, by saying that as long as the people remained loyal to him, everything would turn out fine. The record of the third interview continues:

> *MacArthur:* It is necessary to ban strictly political strikes. But I believe the Japanese are studying democratic principles by engaging in all sorts of activities. . . . If a dangerous situation should arise, I shall immediately confer with you. I do not believe there is a dangerous situation confronting us at present, and I do not think such a situation will break out in the future. I say this because the healthy situation that prevails among the Japanese people is demonstrated by the unswerving respect and affection they have for you. This is proof that the Japanese people will not turn to the destructive extremism of the left.
>
> *Emperor:* Your comments have been truly helpful. As you know, I earnestly wish to go on a national tour but I have held back until the

---

*See Kodama Takanari, "Kimi wa Tennō o Mita ka?" ("Did You See the Emperor?" Tokyo: Asahi Shuppansha, 1975).

constitution has been framed. Some people suggest that I should delay the tour further. What is your opinion?

MacArthur: Whenever you have the opportunity to do so, I believe you should. I think the more often you go on tour, the better it is. Countries like Russia and Australia that want to destroy Japan completely are opposed to your tours, but America and England welcome the idea of your going out among the people. As far as GHQ is concerned you have the freedom to do whatever you wish."*

As this account indicates, the emperor's regional tours had the backing of General MacArthur's headquarters. The emperor visited MacArthur eleven times, and they evidently devoted a considerable portion of their discussions to high-level state policy. The emperor's deep involvement in state affairs at that time was largely because of his usefulness as a conservative bulwark against the rising popularity of communism.

The emperor's involvement in politics is clear from both the nature of his national tours and from the message on Okinawa that he sent to William Sebald at GHQ. It was long thought that the idea of offering Okinawa to the United States originated with the emperor's close advisers, who hoped to keep him from being prosecuted at the Tokyo trials, but that the bargain did not reflect the emperor's wishes. After the emperor passed away, however, Grand Chamberlain Iriye released the entire text of his diary to the public, and the September 20, 1947, entry clearly states: "In accordance with the personal wishes of His Majesty, I sent Terasaki Hidenari to MacArthur. It has to do with the matter of Okinawa." Thus, it was the emperor's personal wish to present the matter to GHQ.

By sending his personal attendant to GHQ to convey his decision on Okinawa, the emperor was not simply acting in the domain of domestic affairs, he was initiating action on major national policy. (The constitution that went into effect in May 1947 strictly prohibits the emperor from taking any action on national policy.) If we apply a favorable interpretation, we can say that the emperor was not yet used to his new, symbolic status. If we view his actions critically, we can suspect that both the United States and the emperor regarded the constitution only as a political device and that, in truth, they did not take it seriously.

The emperor's activities seem to indicate that he was unable to reconcile himself to the fact that he was no longer a sovereign head of state who

---

*Court attendant Terasaki Hidenari's account of Emperor Hirohito's meetings with General MacArthur is in the Shidehara Archives of the National Diet Library.

wielded governing authority. Many other examples of the emperor's interest in national policy appear in Iriye's diary, Kinoshita Michio's *Sokkin Nisshi (Diary of an Imperial Attendant),* and in the *Ashida Hitoshi Nikki (Ashida Hitoshi Diary,* written by the prime minister from March to October 1948).* But after the San Francisco Peace Treaty was signed in 1951, Emperor Hirohito began to refrain from speaking out on state affairs. With this in mind, the next chapter examines the symbolic role of the postwar emperor in Japanese political and cultural life and the changes in the imperial court under the new constitution.

Ashida Hitoshi Nikki, 7 vols. (Tokyo: Iwanami Shoten, 1986).

Chapter 4

THE SYMBOLIC EMPEROR

THE IMPERIAL COURT UNDER
THE NEW CONSTITUTION

Transition to Civil Society

For several years in the immediate postwar period the emperor, as we have seen, went down into the coal mines, to the very ends of the shafts where coal was mined. He went to outlying, isolated mountain and fishing villages, walked along hilly footpaths and called out to old people and children. Then, only twenty years later, he became unreachable—a media figure in a glamorous world beyond the reach of ordinary citizens. The emperor's trips around the country now seem like a relic from a distant time and place. In a transformation that took place in step with Japan's high-speed economic growth, common people lost the ability to approach the emperor, and the emperor was surrounded by a new postwar aristocracy, like a wall around the imperial court.

In looking back over the postwar relationship between the emperor and the people, the fifteen years from 1945, the year of Japan's defeat in the war, to 1960 witnessed an important transition in the emperor's role, from the prewar charismatic wielder of authority to his softer image as a member of civil society. The event that firmly fixed this new image was the marriage in 1959 of the crown prince and the commoner Shōda Michiko. The royal wedding took place at a time of rapid economic growth, when the public was intoxicated with the great economic prosperity of the Iwato Boom.

Shortly after the marriage, in 1960, Japan endured a wave of protests against the renewal of the 1951 Japan-U.S. Mutual Security Pact, which was designed to ensure Japan's protection from communist incursions. Nonetheless, economic growth continued to progress smoothly in the early 1960s.

Successfully winning the honor of hosting the 1964 Olympics in Tokyo led to numerous spin-off projects, such as the new high-speed bullet trains, a network of expressways, jumbo jets, business conglomerates, giant sports stadiums, high-rise building complexes, and so on. These projects were capped by the Osaka International Exposition of 1970, which prompted yet another round of large construction projects. In this period the Tōkaidō-Nagoya-Kobe and Sanyō expressways and coastal factory complexes were completed. Real economic growth rose above ten percent annually during this period, and in some years it approached twenty percent—a spectacular rate.

In this climate of economic expansion, the emperor and the imperial family enjoyed an increasingly glamorous and resplendent new lifestyle in a new royal palace. They became a symbol of worship for the Japanese people, dreaming of unending upward mobility. The new, postwar symbolic emperor's transformation to a civil persona was successful largely thanks to the extraordinary success of Japanese capitalism, but also thanks to the Japanese media.

Making the Imperial Family Fashionable

Media coverage of the imperial family in Japan seems to go in cycles, with periods of intense coverage of the emperor alternating with reporting on other imperial family members, most notably the crown prince. From 1947 to 1950, the emperor was in the public eye almost constantly, though the most intense coverage came much later, in 1989, when the emperor was dying. News reports about the emperor were relatively few during the latter half of the 1950s, when the economy started heating up, and the early 1960s, when the movement against the renewal of the Japan-U.S. Mutual Security Pact was strong.

The marriage of the crown prince in 1959 put him and his commoner wife, Princess Michiko, in the spotlight. Almost all the weekly magazines issued special editions for the occasion; their photo sections were filled with pictures and even more news stories than the daily newspapers published about the event.

Hirohito returned to the spotlight with the 1964 Tokyo Olympics and the early years of high-speed economic growth. With the economy rapidly heading toward the triumphant Iwato Boom, the emperor declared the opening of the games and, with well-orchestrated fanfare, reappeared on the world stage as the leader of a fully rehabilitated Japan.

Shortly after, in 1968 and 1969, students rose up again against the Japan-U.S. Mutual Security Pact and Japan's complicity in the Vietnam War. Their protests caused turmoil throughout the land. During this period, the number of news reports about the emperor dropped significantly and the imperial family as a whole came on stage as the "royal family." They were portrayed as the model of white-collar domesticity and of what became known as "my family-ism." Elegant and refined, with a deep interest in charitable undertakings, the royal family loved sports and were up-to-date on high fashion—in short, an ideal family model for the nation. The focus was not on the crown prince or Princess Michiko as individuals but on the crown prince's family as a whole, including the royal grandchildren, who were depicted as growing up in a happy family environment. At the same time, a new imperial mansion was completed, and the imperial family was seen residing in their beautiful new home. They were proudly touted as part of a prosperous Japan, a magnificent accessory and symbol to be admired.

The weekly magazines contributed more actively than the daily newspapers in both the number of reports and their persistence. Of course, the implicit "chrysanthemum taboo" (a reference to the chrysanthemum symbol used on the imperial seal) against reporting anything critical of the throne had to be observed, so coverage was superficial. However, people began to perceive the negative effects of this media production on the imperial family when Princess Michiko suddenly became wan and careworn.

Nonetheless, coverage of the emperor peaked again when he visited the United States in 1975. This trip was covered more heavily than Emperor Hirohito's European visit in 1971, and it came at a time when the imperial court's role in Japan's foreign relations was most resplendent. Beginning with Queen Elizabeth's visit in 1975, a parade of foreign heads of state came to Japan. This international prominence, in addition to the national celebration of the fiftieth anniversay of his reign in 1976, gave the emperor high public visibility. Then reports about the emperor became relatively few until the news of his critical illness broke in 1989, launching the curve suddenly upward again.

In contrast, the crown prince's popularity peaked about the time of his wedding and declined swiftly from the later years of the 1960s. Popular attention turned to the emperor's grandchildren, Prince Hiro and Prince Aya. As news reports about the emperor and the crown prince became time-worn and their popularity declined, substitute players like the royal grandchildren and potential royal brides surfaced in the media. Thus a highly effective stage presentation unfolded: imperial family members somehow repeatedly appeared in close-up photos, always looking glamorous lest they slip from public attention. At the outset, imperial family advisers like Koizumi Shinzō (1888–1966, one of Crown Prince Akihito's former tutors) probably directed the campaign to put a fashionable public face on the imperial family. Later, however, the media, in cooperation with the Imperial Household Agency, developed and disseminated this new image.

Initially, the Imperial Household Agency sought to restrict the coverage of the royal family and asked the mass media to limit it. But this policy changed as the agency, evidently realizing that fashion would be the mark of the new Japan, set out to remake the imperial family. This new image was epitomized by the coverage of the royal wedding and the accompanying glowing reports on the imperial household. This kind of media coverage not only gave the imperial family a modern image and brought them close to the people, it also stimulated consumer spending and boosted the economy. Beginning in 1959, when the crown prince got married, sales of media-related items like color televisions and magazines rocketed. Spending on other consumer goods, such as clothing, increased as well.

Indeed, the imperial family and the media have a synergistic effect on consumers. For example, in 1975, as part of the foreign policy function of the imperial court, a banquet featuring fine French cuisine was held in honor of Queen Elizabeth. Shortly after, all the high-class French restaurants in the city were jammed with customers. At the 1986 celebration of the sixtieth anniversary of the emperor's reign, Prime Minister Nakasone shouted, "Long live the emperor!" and had gold commemorative coins issued. And people were enthralled.

It is often claimed that the Japanese mass media observe several taboos. These include, most importantly, the chrysanthemum taboo, but also a taboo against reporting discrimination against Japan's outcastes, the *burakumin* (a class of people who have been discriminated against since prefeudal times). The mass media thus refrain from reporting in a critical, analytical fashion about the two groups at opposite social poles—the people with Japan's highest aristocratic status and those at the bottom, whose social status makes them the victims of discrimination. In reporting on the imperial family, the mass media has performed amazing acts of prestidigitation to keep them at the highest level and hold the people's fascination. This treatment, I believe, is a conscious observance of the chrysanthemum taboo.

Becoming the Head of State

The relationship between the emperor and the people began to change in the 1970s, as student activism declined and the International Exposition opened in Osaka. The image of the emperor as a head of state with an illustrious authority developed. Once again, people were proud of the nobility, perceived as having Japan's most ancient bloodline and most exalted cultural traditions. The impression that the emperor was Japan's head of state was made both at home and abroad and was strengthened by Prime Minister Nakasone's controversial official worship in 1985 at Yasukuni Shrine (a Shintō shrine to the war dead) and his repeated sponsorship of state ceremonies honoring the emperor. Detailed cabinet reports on government affairs were written on special paper, wrapped in purple silk cloth, and respectfully sent to the emperor.

Had these actions occurred during the prewar years, when the emperor was a sovereign political authority, no one would have been surprised. But in an era when the emperor was not supposed to be involved in affairs of state, individual cabinet members nonetheless went to the imperial court to keep him informed. These officials referred to themselves not as state ministers but as the emperor's *daijin* (a term used for the heads of government ministries; literally, "a chief subject of the emperor"). The tendency to treat the emperor as Japan's head of state thus developed in the mid-1970s and the public gradually became accustomed to the practice.

The Foreign Ministry in particular clearly indicated to other nations that the emperor should be considered Japan's sovereign. Normally, foreign ambassadors present their credentials to the prime minister, the sovereign representative of the Japanese people, who then reports this to the emperor, the symbol of the state. But the Foreign Ministry began to skip this procedure and brought all new ambassadors directly to the emperor, thus indicating that the emperor was the head of state for purposes of foreign affairs.

At the entrances of Japanese embassy buildings abroad, visitors are greeted by the image of the chrysanthemum seal, the imperial symbol. The receiving rooms contain large photographs of the emperor and empress, but not the prime minister. The cups, saucers, and spoons brought in to serve guests feature the chrysanthemum seal. The impression that the imperial family holds sovereign authority had been created by conservatives in the Foreign Ministry who acted unconstitutionally and without the consent of the Japanese public.

The emperor's image in postwar Japan can thus be divided into three periods: the transition period of fifteen years (1945–1960) in which the emperor system changed from a military institution to a civil one; another fifteen-year period (1960–1975) in which the settled imperial family was displayed to the public as a glamorous example on which citizens could model their pursuit of "my-home-ism"; and, finally, the period from the mid-1970s, when the emperor was transformed into the head of state while ascending fashionably to a world far above ordinary people.

The Imperial Court's Foreign Policy

On September 27, 1971, the emperor and empress took a seven-nation tour of Europe. For the emperor, the trip undoubtedly inspired fond recollections of his European journey of fifty years before.

On their first night in England, the imperial couple was welcomed by Queen Elizabeth and Prince Philip at Buckingham Palace. They traveled the streets of London in a horse-drawn carriage and the emperor appeared delighted. But mean-spirited tabloids like *The London Mail* reported that the citizens of London responded "with an ominous silence, as if they were witnessing a state funeral."

In France, the emperor expressed his appreciation at a luncheon banquet held in his honor at the Elysée Palace by President Pompidou. In West Germany, he shook hands with the president. In Belgium, the imperial couple celebrated with their fellow royal monarchs, the king and queen, at the royal palace in Brussels. In Holland, however (according to *The Telegraph*), a thermos was thrown at Emperor Hirohito's limousine and the glass window was smashed. This act was in protest of the emperor's failure to apologize for the deaths of 19,000 Dutch soldiers in Japanese internment camps during the Second World War. This incident went unreported in Japan, and the Japanese people were led to believe that the emperor had received a rousing welcome from the Europeans wherever he went.

In 1973, Japanese-Chinese relations were restored. The following year the emperor and empress celebrated their golden anniversary in good health. In September 1975, the emperor suddenly made his first television appearance—not on Japanese TV, but on NBC's *Today* show. The Japanese people were perplexed by this decision, but just a week later, the emperor embarked on his long hoped-for visit to the United States.

At the White House dinner welcoming him the emperor said, "The reason I had wished to visit your country for a long time was because . . . I wanted personally to express my gratitude to your people for the warm goodwill and assistance that your country extended to us in helping us rebuild our country immediately after the unfortunate war."

After making this speech, the emperor continued this "goodwill tour" in high spirits, laughing cheerfully and displaying a side of his personality never seen in Japan. The childlike gaiety he displayed at Disneyland was seen in Japanese television broadcasts, creating confusion among many Japanese, who once again felt a deep gulf separating them from the emperor.

Upon his return to Japan on October 31, 1975, the emperor held his first press conference. It was conducted at the imperial palace and lasted only thirty minutes. When asked about the atomic bombing of Japan, the emperor responded, "I regret it, but it was wartime. I felt sorry [for the victims] but I believe it was unavoidable." His response shocked many, including the victims of the bomb. When questioned regarding his responsibility for the war, the emperor replied that he could not answer.

In 1976, the emperor turned seventy-five, and on December 10 of that year a ceremony was held to celebrate his fiftieth year on the throne. During those fifty years, Emperor Hirohito had met countless monarchs, presidents, prime ministers, and high-ranking government officials from around the world—all of whom came and went. Some were removed from their throne or office, some were killed, some were driven from power, some got ill and died. The procession of leaders is a testament to the turbulent course of history in those fifty years.

In the 1970s, because of Japan's rising international status, heads of state from abroad came to Japan even more frequently. American presidents Ford and Carter, Queen Elizabeth of Great Britain, Deng Xiaoping of China, and Prime Minster Feng of Taiwan all spoke with the emperor. Many of the high-ranking foreign officials wanted to meet the emperor out of interest and curiosity, but after the meetings they were highly complimentary about Emperor Hirohito. They described him as a simple, selfless person and as a gentleman who carried himself with natural dignity.

The Japanese people, however, did not unanimously support the emperor and the emperor system. Some, unwilling to forgive the emperor for his responsibility for the war, called for the system's abolition. They criticized the logic of allowing this institution of privilege to survive in a democratic society and pointed to its negative effects on the ethical and educational health of the nation. But the vast majority of the Japanese people accepted the emperor system, and as long as they continue to do so, the system is not likely to disappear.

Somber Self-Restraint and the Mass Media

When the emperor became critically ill in 1988, the Japanese people naturally had a wide range of reactions. The mass media, however, ignored this diversity and, as if in a panic, presented a one-dimensional picture of a nation in a state of somber self-restraint. But even with the approach of X-day (as the day of the emperor's inevitable death was called), a large segment of the Japanese populace remained unruffled. Some, especially students and young people in their teens and twenties, showed a cool indifference, completely at odds with the mood depicted in the mass media.

The significance of this phenomemon was either missed or deliberately ignored by the media—an example of the chrysanthemum taboo against criticizing the emperor. The media vigil around the dying emperor revealed the character of the relationship between the mass media and the emperor. The Imperial Household Agency went to extraordinary lengths to accommodate media coverage, allowing over a thousand reporters to crowd into the agency compounds. When the weather turned cold, the agency built a tent village so that the press corps could maintain all-night vigils to report even the slightest change in the emperor's condition. To back up the usual reporters, other correspondents from all over the nation were brought in for support. No detail was to be missed. This extraordinary phenomenon continued for about a hundred days.

For two weeks after the emperor had begun coughing blood (on September 19), the mass media suppressed any critical comments about the emperor or the emperor system. Perhaps this kind of censorship is to be expected of NHK, Japan's quasi-governmental public network, but private broadcasting networks and the major newspapers also failed to report any critical comments. Perhaps they were afraid of being labeled "un-Japanese" or perhaps they believed that the entire Japanese population was uniformly in a state of sorrow.

The demeanor of the mass media during Emperor Hirohito's illness and death was reminiscent of the wartime media's response to the outbreak of total war with China in 1937 (which they called "a holy war for peace in Asia" and "a war to chastise China"). At that time, the mass media as well as the conservative parties preserved the general climate of opinion that did not permit any criticism of the war. Unfortunately, as demonstrated by the media during the emperor's illness, these wartime habits have survived into the postwar era.

Why does the right wing in Japan become violently agitated whenever anyone criticizes the emperor and commit acts of terror, rejecting all rational discourse? When Fukazawa Shichirō published his "Fūryū Mutan" ("Elegant Tales of Dreams") in Chūō Kōron magazine in February, 1961, right-wing activists, accusing Chūō Kōron of insulting the emperor, attacked the home of the magazine's president and killed two people. More recently, the mayor of Nagasaki, Motoshima Hitoshi, was shot on January 18, 1990, for commenting, in response to a question, "The emperor, too, is responsible for the war." Even critical comments made by small citizens' circles have resulted in threatening phone calls and constant harassment.

In this climate of intimidation, all the mass media exercised self-restraint by limiting entertainment programming upon Emperor Hirohito's death and during the "ceremony of national mourning." In this case, however, many listeners and viewers protested vociferously and the period of self-restraint was reduced from three days to only a day and a half. The entertainment programs resumed their normal schedule after three days. This public response was a reaction against the mass media's arbitrary monopoly and control of information, which had been so evident while the emperor was critically ill in the previous year.

But this reaction was mostly on the part of the young and cannot be ascribed to the population as a whole. For those over fifty, in particular various leaders in the society, the reaction was different. The emperor system is deeply rooted in the intellectual and spiritual makeup of Japanese who were born before the war. Indeed, the emperor system is inherently an intellectual-spiritual framework. To fully understand that framework, however, it is helpful to consider two examples from the postwar years that represent the spiritual relationship between the emperor and the people.

THE EMPEROR SYSTEM AS A SPIRITUAL FRAMEWORK

Long Live the Emperor!

Ishimure Michiko's documentary masterpiece Kugai Jōdo (Paradise in the Sea of Sorrow)* tells of the suffering caused by the Minamata industrial mercury poisoning, which happened in the mid-1950s. The book concerns a patient named Sakanoue Yuki, the most seriously afflicted Minamata disease victim. Sakanoue Yuki, a fisherwoman, had worked with her husband in Yatsushiro Bay in the Shiranui Sea. When she was stricken by

---

*Tokyo: Kōdansha, 1969. The subtitle of the English edition, published in 1990 by Yamaguchi (Kyoto), is Our Minamata Disease.

Minamata disease, she lost the ability to move her hands and legs. Yuki asked for help from doctors, prefectural and city pollution management committees, and relatives—all to no avail. They dismissed her, and some even accused her of trying to profit financially from the situation. In the end, she was abandoned even by her husband and consigned to a corner of the hospital.

In September 1968, Minister of Welfare Sonoda Sunao came to Minamata and visited the Minamata Municipal Hospital. The seriously ill Minamata disease patients in Sakanoue Yuki's ward were told in advance of the minister's impending visit and anxiously awaited his arrival. When Sonoda entered the ward, Yuki underwent a muscular convulsion and shouted, "Long live the emperor!" Then, gasping, she sang the national anthem and began to cry aloud. Yuki's behavior seemed odd and surprising to the government officials, who quickly left the room.

Sakanoue Yuki had began to fantasize that the only person who could help her was the emperor. But the emperor in Sakanoue Yuki's mind was not the real emperor, but the ideal of a kind, noble ruler. When she was young, all girls were taught the spirit of militarism. The ruler was the "Son of Heaven," a living god who viewed all Japanese people with equal compassion. Though we cannot know exactly what kind of superior being she embraced in her heart, she perhaps thought her great savior finally had sent a cabinet minister to her. So the words "Long live the emperor!" and the national anthem ("May His Majesty's reign last a thousand years, eight thousand years") no doubt burst out instinctively.

In 1968, Japan's economy was at the peak of its high-speed growth period. Japan took great pride in the fact that its GNP had surpassed West Germany's, making Japan an economic power second only to the United States in the noncommunist world. Also at that time, the young began to perceive the contradictions in postwar Japanese society, and protest movements in the academic world spread throughout the land. Sakanoue Yuki's cry symbolized the plight of the forsaken of postwar Japan—those brought up under the wartime imperial system who could not shake it off.

Popular nationalism in Japan is often triggered by the fervor of the public, who, when desperate (as they were several times during the Shōwa era), unconsciously search for a salvation beyond their own narrow lives or villages. For some salvation may be a world of the Maitreya, the compassionate future Buddha, who will come to save the world. Others may yearn for an ideal world in which society has been reconstructed along more equitable lines. But when the search for an answer focuses on the present world, it often becomes a nationalistic aspiration that incorporates emperor worship. Sakanoue Yuki, left alone to suffer and die, could deal with her deep bitterness only by fantasizing about an absolute power who would save her. At such points of desperation, Japanese people traditionally turn their fantasies into emperor worship or popular religious cults. This phenomenon is frightening, but popular nationalism frequently comes from such an extreme psychological state.

Generally speaking, this type of nationalism is different from state or imperial nationalism, which are imposed from above. Instead, it is a kind of fantasy of community, a consciousness directed toward the external world as people's social perspective extends from the village to the prefecture, from the prefecture to the nation, and from the nation to the world. The Japanese people's unfulfilled aspiration for freedom of social consciousness is the core of this kind of popular nationalism.

The Abandoned Soldiers and the Emperor

A second symbolic example of the relationship between the emperor and the people is the case of the Japanese soldiers who had been abandoned overseas after Japan's surrender in the Second World War. In January 1972, twenty-eight years after the end of the war, a former Japanese soldier was rescued from a cave in the jungle on the island of Guam. Former Corporal Yokoi Shōichi, fifty-six years old, had excellent survival skills. An ordinary person probably would have surrendered or gone insane from the fear and isolation. But Yokoi stubbornly survived alone. A tailor in Nagoya before the war, he could make his own shoes, his own clothing, ropes, and so on—more than eighty items necessary for daily life. The Japanese people were deeply impressed by his ability to survive.

Upon returning to Japan, Yokoi said, "I am ashamed to say that I returned home having prolonged my life. For twenty-eight years I stayed alive by enduring hardship and pain."

The phrase, "I am ashamed" surprised people and even became a popular saying that year. These words were long-forgotten. Toward whom did he feel this sense of shame? He said, "I brought back with me the rifle that I had reverently received from the emperor . . . I am returning this to His Majesty. I am ashamed that I failed to serve His Majesty one hundred percent."

The fervent sentiment revealed in this statement enabled him to survive alone for so many years. Yokoi's concept of "His Majesty" was no doubt finely purified and fantasized. Later, after he realized what had happened in Japan since the war, Corporal Yokoi remarked, "I wasted half of my life."

Nonetheless, shouldn't it have been "His Majesty" who truly felt shame when confronted with this pure, innocent sentiment from a common Japanese citizen? He did not utter a word of thanks to people like Yokoi who had suffered hardship and pain (those "heroic spirits" who died in the jungle).

Corporal Yokoi returned to Japan in February 1972, an extraordinary time for the nation. People were swept up by a media frenzy surrounding the police raid on the Red Army Faction's hideout at a lodge on Mt. Asama. All the TV stations were competing to deliver the dramatic news, making live broadcasts from the scene of the gun battle.

Two years later, in March 1974, Second-Lieutenant Onoda Hirō appeared, this time out of the jungles of Lubang Island in the Philippines. Onoda had continued fighting for thirty years as an intelligence agent "left behind." A year and a half before, Onoda's subordinate, army Private First Class Kozuka Kinshichi, had died in combat with the local police force. Onoda and others were members of a special intelligence-gathering corps. They knew that Japan had lost the war, but continued to fight because they had not received any orders relieving them of their duties. In order to perform their duty, they moved from place to place in the jungle with their possessions on their backs. Onoda, governed by a stern military spirit, refused to lay down his sword or rifle until he received a direct order to surrender from his immediate superior officer, Major Taniguchi. As a result, the former major had to fly to the Philippines to order Onoda to surrender. Thereupon Onoda surrendered to the local army commander.

The people of Japan were surprised and struck by Onoda's rectitude. He considered himself "a one-man Japanese army," exemplifying the spirit of the imperial forces. Because this attitude was so far removed from the reality of postwar Japan, his sudden appearance caused heated discussion about Japanese society and the emperor. Some saw Onoda's attitude as striking evidence of how fiercely the emperor system had gripped the minds and spirits of the people. The Japanese reaction to the return of these two men was complex; people felt surprise, respect, befuddlement, and shock at remembering what had been long forgotten.

In contrast to the enthusiastic welcome of these two men, however, the Japanese government and people were extremely cold toward another returning former soldier, Nakamura Teruo. Nakamura, like the other two soldiers, suffered for decades as he carried on in the name of the emperor. Like the other two cases, his return revealed part of the legacy of the wartime emperor system. The reason for his cold reception was, quite simply, that he was born not in Japan but in the former Japanese colony of Taiwan.

These soldiers, like the terribly stricken Sakanoue Yuki and many others, were some of modern Japan's forsaken subjects of the great Japanese empire.

The External Structure of Imperial Rule

While the emperor system still is embedded deeply in the hearts of the Japanese people, it remains fluid, with each new generation of Japanese forming different nuances and images of it. Some consider the system as more of a cultural than a political entity, for example, and some regard it as a civil institution. The emperor system thus has a particular psychological place in Japan, where people continue to look up to the emperor with a special feeling of reverence. Despite the dissenters, such sentiments still are very much alive.

The emperor system can be divided, roughly, into its external and internal aspects. The external structure was first analyzed in 1932 by the Marxist scholars known as the Kōzaha Faction (literally, the lectures faction, a group that argued that the Meiji Restoration did not end feudalism, but instead produced an absolutist emperor system underpinned by a semifeudal landholding system). The Kōzaha Faction believed that the characteristics and organization of the governing system instituted by the Meiji Constitution had gone through several different stages. Essentially, the emperor had absolute authority in all areas as imperial sovereign. As the commander-in-chief of the army and navy, he held absolute authority over the military. As leader of the Diet, he held the right to issue imperial decrees. He also held the constitutional right to appoint judicial and administrative officials. That the emperor held these powers formally was primary; whether he used them was secondary.

The emperor was at the top of the pyramidal governing structure, and directly under him were the aristocrats, referred to as the *hanpei* (the palace guard). Among the aristocrats, in addition to the royalty, were the former *daimyō* (lords) of the Tokugawa regime, who had become counts and viscounts after the Meiji Restoration, and the very rich, including some landowners and capitalists, who had become barons. These groups constituted the ruling strata, protecting the prestige of the imperial house.

The next level down in this structure was the bureaucratic apparatus consisting of imperial appointees in three categories: *chokunin, sōnin, and hannin* (direct imperial appointees, appointees with imperial sanction, and junior appointees). At the bottom of this pyramid were the prominent local families who served as town and village heads. They had daily contact with the people and transmitted commands from above.

Under this pyramidal prewar governing system, the emperor was not a neutral or detached entity that transcended the class structure; his domination of the class structure was rigidly enforced. The system included a tight nationwide network of police headquarters and local police stations, as well as the powerful thought police, who constantly spied upon and pursued suspicious persons.

If these factors were the only features of the system, the people at the bottom layer certainly would have become embittered. But the emperor system was designed to deflect their bitterness. What factors helped it succeed? When we look at the other side of this hard, external structure, we find the softer components of the emperor system.

The Other Side of Benevolence Toward All

The flip side of the external structure of the emperor system also featured the emperor as a transcendent entity, at or above the summit of the system. Underneath him were many layers of classes, with the outcaste *burakumin* (several million people in several thousand communities) at the bottom. The emperor was outside the controlling power structure, not directly linked to the framework.

This arrangement was very clever. Below even the discriminated-against *burakumin,* at the bottommost level of society, were other groups like the Okinawans, the Koreans, the aboriginal Ainu and other minorities. The emperor, in his detached, lofty position, could be seen as benevolent by all. This fantasy was stronger among those most distant from the emperor. This system was based on a psychological framework that focused the hopes and fantasies of the most desperate people on the emperor, situated at the transcendent summit but not tangibly connected to the power structure. By maintaining this purely spiritual connection, the emperor, together with the bourgeoisie and land-owning classes, could skirt their responsibility and avoid the threat of being overthrown.

Why, for example, did the people of Okinawa fight to the end, organize special combat battalions, and commit mass suicide, dying with shouts of "Long live the emperor!"? This behavior cannot be explained simply in terms of their childhood indoctrination as loyal imperial subjects. Many other reasons lie behind these actions, but in the Okinawans' hearts was a fantasized concept of the emperor.

The emperor system was organized so that the hard, external side of the power structure—the special higher police, the military police, the Peace Preservation Laws, and the other forces used to intimidate and discriminate against the lower classes—was covered up by the gentler side. If the internal side of the system offered solace and hope to the people at the bottom, then the external aspect was the ruling structure based on discrimination and control. This external framework was strenuously concealed from the people, who were presented with a facade of relief and salvation. This deceitful ideology was a frightening trap for those on the bottom.

In its essence, the emperor system was the structural regime of discrimination and control that supported the ruling classes of that period. During the war, a small minority benefited from this system, while the vast majority of the remaining populace endured extreme hardship or were sacrificed to the war. Despite this suffering, the people mostly continued to fantasize that they had been recipients of the emperor's love, his divine "benevolence toward all." They were consoled by the belief that if the emperor bowed reverently to the war dead at Yasukuni Shrine, their husbands and sons who had perished in the war would gain salvation.

It is said that in his regional travels the emperor went into the tenement houses and deep into the mines, saying things like, "It may be difficult, but do your best," "Work hard for the goal of rebuilding Japan," and "So your father died. How is your mother? Now, do your best." People were profoundly moved when they heard that the emperor had spoken this way. The psychological legacy of the prewar emperor system occasionally is still quite visible. It explains why so many (especially older) Japanese maintained a somber state of self-restraint and quiescence during the emperor's critical illness in 1988.

The Emperor System Will Change

The postwar generations' concept of the emperor system is very different from that of the prewar generation. I conducted several surveys of about five-hundred of my students when the emperor became ill, when he passed away, and during the time of national mourning. I found their thoughts about the emperor to be surprisingly cool and indifferent.

A number of students said that the emperor is necessary for Japan, though their definition of necessary differs from that of the older generation. The students felt that Japan needs the imperial family because they are the only Japanese who have remained loyal to tradition and who have a clearcut ancestry. Therefore, they felt, the imperial family is important and should not be sealed off from the public. The students thought that the royal family should appear openly in public, no matter what the expense.

Some said that the emperor was a terrific person: he had lots of money, lived in a spacious mansion, was the most famous person in Japan and, after all, met Japan's most talented people once a year (when even the stars would turn humble and timid before him). These students also said that they wouldn't want to be members of the royal family, to have no freedom, and have attendants follow them wherever they go. Yet these same people say the emperor system is necessary.

When I asked them why so many young people signed the memorial register at the imperial palace as Emperor Hirohito lay ill, they replied that many people thought, "Now that I'm here I might as well write down the names of all my family members." Participation in this event was free and, after all, one might by chance appear on television. Many felt that the change from the Shōwa to the Heisei era (as the reign of Emperor Akihito is named) was historically significant and signed their names to the register as if stamping a memorial seal: "It'll be part of history." This perception of the emperor system is completely different than that of the older generation. The young generations today no longer think that the apex of life would be to ride in the golden palanquin.

The mass media failed to report this reaction on the part of the younger generations. Instead, the newspapers and televisions were filled with reports of "one hundred million people in a state of subdued restraint and mourning." The media claimed that the whole nation was saturated with affection and respect for the emperor, when actually a strong element of the conventional Japanese behavior was at work: go because everybody else is going.

Even though many young people might approve of the emperor system, as younger generations take over society, the general concept of the emperor will be quite different from that of earlier generations. When asked if the emperor system is necessary, today's young people tend to say things like, "It's not necessary to get rid of it," "It doesn't hurt to keep the system," and "Japan has so much money anyway, so it's all right to let those people live in luxury." The young don't view the emperor with the traditional respect and affection—they think of the emperor as being equal to themselves. They do not perceive the emperor system in a hierarchical sense, and thus they feel that the members of the royal family should get closer to the people.

Though aristocrats and media stars invited to royal garden parties still shrink with humility when the emperor speaks to them, the young consider the imperial family to be human beings. Young people envy royalty because they are privileged, have lots of money, and live well; but they also pity the royal family because they are always surrounded by people and have no freedom. Thus, young people perceive the royal family simply as citizens of a civil society.

Before long, most of the population will feel this way, so the role of the imperial family is bound to change accordingly. During the Meiji era, the people viewed themselves in relation to a supposedly unchanging imperial family. But after the defeat in the war, the imperial family began to adjust to the the prevailing social trends. Of course, there was great debate when Crown Prince Akihito and later his second son, Prince Akishino, married commoners, and both of these young women were idolized by the public. But today the people constitute the center of power and the imperial court must adjust to the attitude of the people. Otherwise, the emperor system will not be able to continue.

Mishima Yukio once lamented, "Why did the *Sumera-mikoto* (an ancient term for the emperor) have to become merely human?" But such reactions to changes in the emperor system have now become a thing of the past. A qualitative change has occurred in the relationship between the emperor and the people. Despite the image conveyed by the media, this change was demonstrated dramatically in the reaction of the people during the period from the time of self-restraint during the emperor's illness to the period of national mourning after his death.

What Did the Emperor Think About the People?

What were Emperor Hirohito's thoughts about the people? After combing through the many historical documents published thus far, I have concluded that the emperor was constantly concerned about the well-being of the people. He worried about them because he firmly believed, during and after the war, that the Japanese people loved him.

John Gunther writes that during the first meeting between Emperor Hirohito and General MacArthur, the emperor said:

My people like me very much. Since they do like me very much, they would simply have locked me up in a lunatic asylum until the war was over, if I had made any protest about the war or worked for peace. If I had done so and they had not liked me very much, they would have cut my throat.*

It is hard to believe that the emperor could have said anything like that to General MacArthur. The emperor's sense of himself was not like the modern concept of the self. He was brought up to believe that he was a link in a single, unbroken lineage that originated in the time of the sun goddess, Amaterasu, and was transmitted through all the later emperors, his imperial ancestors. Thus the emperor's place was firm and unique. Naturally, his primary concern would be the imperial throne that had been handed down through the ages. The Shōwa emperor felt he had a mission to preserve the imperial line, protect the ancient sacred treasures, and pass them on to his descendants. Undoubtedly, these goals meant the preservation of the national polity.

The national polity could not be sustained without the loyal support of the Japanese people. Thus, the emperor naturally felt affection for the people and thought about their welfare from the bottom of his heart: the people upheld the system that supposedly had continued unbroken since ancient times. So for the sake of the people the emperor would sometimes endure pain, but sacrificing his life would mean the destruction of the national polity. Thus there was a limit to what he could do "for the sake of the people."

Preserving the National Polity

In August 1945, when Japan accepted the terms of the Potsdam Declaration, the emperor's foremost concern was how to preserve the national polity. He states in his *Soliloquy:*

At that time my first concern was the people, for if the existing conditions continued they would be destroyed. I would not be able to protect the people, my children. Secondly . . . if the enemy were to land in the vicinity of Ise Bay, the two shrines of Ise and Atsuta would fall im-

*John Gunther, *The Riddle of MacArthur* (New York: Harper & Brothers, 1950), p. 116.

mediately under enemy control. We would not have the time to move the imperial treasures; we would not be able to protect them. If that were to happen it would be difficult to preserve the national polity. Thus, I decided that we must negotiate for peace even if I had to sacrifice my own life.

The emperor did not strenuously oppose war with China because there was little fear that Japan would lose. There was no threat to the national polity or to the imperial throne, so he took a rather open position toward war with China and ignored the activities of the military. But when the military proposed war against the United States and Great Britain, there was danger that Japan could lose the war. In this case, as embodied in the emperor system, the national polity might be destroyed by the victor nations. Toward the end of the war, when this sense of crisis grew acute, the emperor strongly advocated peace, though this opinion evidently did not spring from pacifist convictions.

At the same time, though, the emperor was not a militarist. Emperor Hirohito had the flexibility to side with whomever the prevailing circumstances favored. He did not possess a subjective sense of the self, ideas, or beliefs. Rather, he lived with a sense of great responsibility to pass on to the next generation the traditions that he had inherited as part of the unbroken lineage from myriads of years past. For this reason, he had a real affection for the people.

The current emperor, Akihito, also has inherited that desire to preserve the imperial traditions. As long as the people do not come into conflict with this fundamental principle, the emperor's love of the people will remain authentic. Thus, to think that Emperor Hirohito decided to end the war for the sake of the people, giving up all other considerations, does not run true to historical reality. His intentions are revealed in the draft of the new year imperial proclamation (the so-called declaration on being human) that was formulated toward the end of 1945.

Descendant of the Gods or Human?

As part of their design for the democratization of Japan, the occupation authorities advised the emperor to refute the myth that he was a descendant of the sun goddess and, therefore, divine. The original draft of the declaration on being human is said to have been written by Prime Minister Shidehara Kijūrō and amended by General MacArthur. According to the December 9 entry in Kinoshita Michio's diary, *Sokkin Nisshi*, the draft reads:

> The ties between me [the emperor] and the people have the distinctive quality of having been bound perennially by mutual trust and love. These ties are not based simply on tradition and myths. This is based on the false notion that the Japanese people [MacArthur changed this to read "emperor"] are descendants of the gods, and that we are superior to other peoples and are destined to rule the world.

The phrase "descendants of the gods" became an issue. Deputy Grand Chamberlain Kinoshita wrote,

> It may be permissible to say that the idea that the Japanese people are descendants of the gods is false but we cannot allow it to be said that the idea that the *emperor* is a descendant of the gods is false. So on my own initiative I decided to change the statement to say that it is a false concept to say that the emperor is a living god.

When Kinoshita asked the emperor's opinion about this rephrasing, "His Majesty agreed with my suggestion. He was opposed to publicizing the idea 'Saying that the emperor is a descendant of the gods is a false concept.'" Thus, in the new draft, it was not the notion of "the emperor as a descendant of the gods" that was described as false, but the *invented* notion of the emperor as "a living god." Simply put, the idea was defended that the emperor is a descendant of the gods. This rephrasing was to be expected because the emperor actually believed that he was a descendant of the sun goddess, Amaterasu. Can this statement truly be called a declaration on being human?

In 1977, over thirty years after the declaration, in an interview with reporters at Nasu, the emperor revealed the truth about the declaration on being human. There were "two issues related to the denial of divine status," he said.

> The first objective of that declaration was to propound an imperial oath. At that time there was a concern that the people would be overwhelmed by powerful foreign forces like America. The adoption of democracy was based on the will of the Meiji emperor, as seen in the Charter Oath of Five Articles. That was a pledge made to the gods by the Great Emperor. There was an urgent need to show that democracy was not an imported concept.

The emperor must have meant article one of the Charter Oath, issued in April 1868: "Deliberative Assemblies shall be widely established and all state affairs decided by public opinion." At the time, the Meiji emperor had just ascended to the throne, a mere youth of sixteen with no political opinions. In light of the circumstances of that period, it is clear that this oath was far removed from real democratic principles.

Was Emperor Hirohito's historical knowledge faulty? The Meiji Constitution, which is regarded as the fulfillment of the Charter Oath of Five Articles, was based on the rejection of the demands by the "people's rights" movement for the establishment of a democratic constitutional monarchy. About sixty-four draft constitutions were formulated by the movement, but the Meiji leaders rejected all of them, oppressed the advocates of democracy, and, without consulting the people, secretly drafted the constitution and promulgated it in the emperor's name. Of course, the Meiji Constitution included provision for a Diet and granted the people the right to examine the budget and approve legislation, but all other political power was lodged in the emperor's sovereign authority.

Subsequently, of course, the power of the political parties increased and the constitutional elements of the Meiji Constitution were expanded by public pressure, such as the Taishō democracy movement in the 1920s and the theory of the emperor as an organ posited by Minobe Tatsukichi and others. But there were limits to these developments. The Meiji Constitution had powerful, absolutist provisions, including the emperor system, that clashed with the principles of a truly democratic constitution. For this reason, in 1935 the Japanese government formally renounced the organ theory, and in 1937 printed hundreds of thousands of copies of a pamphlet entitled "Fundamentals of Our National Polity," which emphasized loyalty to the emperor, patriotism, filial piety, social harmony, self-sacrifice, and the martial spirit while urging citizens to reject individualism, socialism, and communism. This pamphlet was distributed to schools throughout the land. If, under these circumstances, Emperor Hirohito believed that he was a constitutional monarch, then he was very isolated indeed.

It thus cannot be argued that Emperor Hirohito had no responsibility for the war because he was a constitutional monarch. The reality in prewar Japan was that the system of constitutional monarchy had weakened and the government had openly rejected this more democratic interpretation of the constitution. The emperor was given supreme authority. Party government ceased in the early 1930s, and in 1940 the political parties were dissolved. In this situation, the concept of constitutional monarchy survived only in the emperor's mind. Even if he still hoped to be like the

British royal court, the political situation was moving away from that concept.

Thus the emperor had the responsibility of taking resolute command of the military and exercising his authority as the commander-in-chief of the armed forces in accordance with provisions of the Meiji Constitution. He also had the responsiblity of providing leadership in the nation's political affairs. He bears a heavy burden for abandoning his constitutional responsibility, remaining in the grip of a fantasy, and mismanaging the political affairs of the nation. Nevertheless, before and after Emperor Hirohito's death, scholars and journalists have ignored this culpability and raced to defend him by arguing that the emperor was a constitutional monarch and therefore not responsible either from the legal or political standpoint.

THE END OF THE SHŌWA ERA

The Paradox of Shōwa Political History

On January 7, 1989, at 6:33 A.M., Emperor Hirohito died, ending a turbulent life of eighty-seven years and eight months. His death came about four months after September 19, 1988, when he threw up a large amount of blood and his critical condition was made public. After further loss of blood and a series of blood transfusions (over 20,000 cc), his condition seemed to improve. As the emperor's condition got better and then worse, the mass media and the general public alternated between relief and concern. But the tense atmosphere at the outset of his illness did not continue for the entire public vigil. By the time emperor's condition became most critical, the frenzy of prayers and the rush of admirers inscribing their names in the imperial logbooks had abated.

But with the long-expected arrival of X-day, as the anticipated day of death was called, the entire nation, spurred on by the government and the mass media, seemed to turn into what someone called "an archipelago of sorrow." The entertainment world was asked to postpone performances, shops were closed, neon signs were turned off, and everyone seemed to abide by the unwritten rules of mourning. Nonetheless, some citizens' groups met to criticize the emperor and some demonstrations were held to protest the government's call for self-restraint.

The emperor's death (given special status by the mass media, which used the unfamiliar term *hōgyo*, "the death of a royal personage") was headline news in the papers that morning. Scholars contributed some interesting commentary about the emperor in the *Asahi Shinbun*, filling all thirteen columns of a two-page centerfold (pages that, rare for Japanese papers, included no advertising). A specialist in modern Japanese history at Tokyo University, Professor Itō Takashi, wrote an essay entitled "The Political Role of the Shōwa Emperor"; a political scientist at Rikkyo University, Professor Takabatake Michitoshi, wrote "The Shōwa Emperor: One Body, Two Lives"; and Professor Takeda Kiyoko of the International Christian University discussed the meaning of Emperor Hirohito's life from the perspective of an intellectual historian.

The intellectual positions of these scholars were well known. The *Asahi Shinbun* obviously sought to present an uncontroversial, balanced view from right-wing and slightly leftist perspectives. The essays evidently were carefully worked over; their styles were flawless. What was surprising was that all three articles defended the Shōwa emperor and agreed that he had no responsibility for the war. Itō Takashi's position as a defender of the emperor was well known, so his essay was no surprise. But Takabatake Michitoshi was a hard-line liberal as a citizen activist during the movements against the Japan-U.S. Mutual Security Pact and the Vietnam War, so his words were surprising indeed. Not wanting to misunderstand his position, I read the article three times, but Takabatake had indeed joined the chorus eulogizing the emperor. I wondered what had led him to such a position.

Before investigating Takabatake's position, I must note the warm sympathy for the emperor shared by all three scholars. They empathized with the emperor's storm-ridden life, sought to understand his life from his point of view, and tried to explain his position. If these experts were ordinary citizens, their position could be viewed as courteous, commendably polite behavior toward someone who had just passed away. But these three analysts undoubtedly had been asked to prepare their comments in advance and had been given the heavy responsibility of representing the best thinking on the subject in Japan. In this case, they could be expected to offer a strictly scholarly, critical stance and not be moved by the moment's sorrow.

Itō Takashi's thesis is that as constitutional monarch, the emperor faithfully abided by the prewar constitutional principles and only "sanctioned the decisions made by legally established government agencies." He was not responsible for the war, and thus there is no reason to pursue the question of his war responsibility. In the postwar period, the emperor performed his duties as the symbol of the Japanese nation. Itō makes a positive assessment of the emperor's role, stating that the Shōwa emperor "contributed to the stability of Japanese society, and to the creation of a favorable image of Japan abroad." Itō's essay contained nothing new; he merely was restating the often-repeated views of the establishment scholars.

Takabatake Michitoshi arrives at similar conclusions, but his argument is more meticulous and his essay is twice as long as Itō's. At first glance, his analysis appears to be balanced, based on a deep understanding of the emperor system. But on further examination, Takabatake's essay reveals its lack of a coherent structure and fails to deal with the emperor's relationship with the people. Instead, he focuses only on the emperor's relationship with the military. The question should have been: Did the emperor consider using his power—based on the people's respect, love, and trust for him—to lead Japan correctly?

Takabatake Michitoshi states:

> Basically we can consider [the emperor] a proponent of peace, a man who emphasized the importance of international cooperation with America and the European nations, and did his utmost to avoid war. Also, he can be seen as the upholder of constitutional principles, and one who respected the constitutionally established government and Diet, and abhorred the ideas of dictatorship and direct imperial rule. The end result of these beliefs was the "sacred decision" to end the war.*

Is this evaluation accurate? It is argued that the emperor consistently was a proponent of peace. But, in reality, he took this position only toward the powerful Western nations—his position toward the weaker Asian nations was quite different. Also, the argument that the emperor behaved according to constitutional principles applies only to his actions on the decisions made by the government and the military. He did not try to implement the will of the people, which constitutes the essence of democracy.

The age of Taishō democracy taught that only popular resistance and public opinion can truly defend democratic constitutional government and suppress the aggressive plans of those wielding power. Did the Shōwa emperor understand this lesson? I believe he did not, because he sanctioned the Peace Preservation Law, which fundamentally endangered democracy, and thus tacitly authorized the power to completely crush the popular movements for freedom of speech, peace, and civil rights. The prewar social scientists of the opposition agreed, whatever faction they be-

---

*Takabatake Michitoshi, *Tōron: Sengo Nihon no Seiji Shisō (Debate: Postwar Japan's Political Thought)* (Tokyo: Sanichi Shobō, 1978.)

longed to, that the dark side of the emperor system was reflected in such acts as the Peace Preservation Law. Takabatake's scholarship seems questionable when he calls the emperor a supporter of constitutionalism while neglecting   these   issues.

Takabatake also wrote:

> The greatest paradox of Shōwa political history lies in the fact that the Shōwa emperor who, as the supreme leader was *outwardly* seen as the person most responsible for the war, was, in his personal sentiments, a proponent of peace who continuously hoped to avoid war.

Was this truly the *greatest* paradox of Shōwa political history? The paradox more accurately resides in the fact that the emperor, who had the absolute support of the Japanese people (and many believed that dying for the sake of the emperor was worthwhile), did not use the people's power. Instead, he was manipulated by a small group of militarists and bureaucrats, all the while bemoaning his isolation?

Takabatake next raises a key question: Why did not the emperor, who prevented a battle in Japan itself and saved the people from destruction, "make use of the power he possessed to move events, that he displayed in his 'sacred decision' to end the war, and prevent the outbreak of either the Fifteen-Year War or the American-Japanese war?" Part of the reason, Takabatake wrote, is that the military leaders caused the emperor to make the wrong judgments.

> But the biggest problem stemmed from the emperor's personal opposition to the thinking of the military extremists and the emperorists, and his desire to remain faithful to the original interpretation and provisos of the Meiji Constitution. Consequently, except for occasions when the governmental functions had been in fact paralyzed, like the time of the February 26th Incident and the end of the war, he seldom sought to actively direct the course of political affairs on the basis of his own judgment.

Thus, Takabatake's explanation is quite similar to Itō Takashi's.

However, it must be stressed that by the outbreak of the Japanese-American War (1941), the emperor's idealistic views of constitutional government had been quashed. The party government system, the pillar of constitutional government, had ceased after the May 15th Incident in 1932 (when radical extremists assassinated Prime Minister Inukai); the organ theory of the emperor system based on constitutional law was formally renounced by the government in 1935; and the political parties and the Diet were transformed into the Imperial Rule Assistance Association in 1940. Constitutionalism had become a mere shell. At that point, citing constitutional principles was a fantasy and could have been useful only as an excuse for the growing dictatorship.

The assertion made by Takabatake and others that the emperor seldom actively sought to direct political affairs also does not square with the facts. The material in Kido Kōichi's diary, the emperor's *Soliloquy*, and other sources reveals that the emperor regularly spoke on political and military matters and to tried to direct events (even though he gave up when things didn't go as he had planned). Can one absolve the emperor of responsibility for these political actions by saying that he was simply behaving as a constitutional monarch?

Takabatake Michitoshi concludes the passage cited previously by stating, "In this respect the emperor himself was a prisoner and victim of the institution of the emperor system and the pressures of the times." If the emperor was a prisoner and victim, what shall we call the many people who were arrested under the Peace Preservation Law and other repressive laws, tortured, condemned as guilty in the name of the emperor, sent to prison, and crippled or killed? Who can be held accountable for the fate of the Koreans, Chinese, and Southeast Asians who were rounded up from the colonies established by Japanese imperialism and forced into service or brutally killed? And what of the several hundred thousand people who died in the battlefields, mumbling "Long live the emperor!"? Do we say that no one was responsible, that the times were at fault, and that the emperor himself was a prisoner and victim of the times? Ultimately, does that reasoning not mean that "all 100 million Japanese must repent" for the crimes Japan committed?

The first article of the Imperial Rescript to Soldiers and Sailors states, "The soldier and sailor should consider loyalty their essential duty." The second article states, "Regard the command of your superior officers as my command." The soldiers and sailors were absolutely forbidden to disobey these injunctions. I find it difficult to imagine that the emperor truly believed his own statement that "I have no responsibility because I was acting as a constitutional monarch."

Of course, the responsibility for the war does not belong to the emperor alone. The senior statesmen, generals, and admirals surrounding the emperor shared the responsibility, as did the men who pushed for war by fanatically glorifying the emperor as a living god and the many midlevel leaders who followed the first group and actively organized and mobilized the masses.

In terms of responsibility for the war, a distinction must be made between the leaders and those who were manipulated by them. Even though they may have acted under the command of their superior officers, many soldiers went beyond the legitimate bounds of self-defense to commit crimes such as murder, rape, and pillage. The specific actions of these soldiers should be condemned in the name of humanity and cannot be forgiven. These crimes cannot be glossed over by slogans like "100 million Japanese repenting together." All Japanese of that time are responsible for the war, though there may be different degrees of culpability. If we Japanese fail to conduct a stringent self-examination, we demonstrate that as a people we are morally flawed. The Japanese failure to do so is seen by other nations as evidence of a decisive difference in the way Japan and Germany—both defeated in the war—have shouldered responsibility for the war. Unless this fundamental flaw is corrected, the Japanese can never develop genuine friendships with peoples of the world. Even though Japan has become the most technologically and economically advanced nation of Asia, it has not won the moral and spiritual respect of other nations.

Reaction from Abroad

While Japanese scholars were actively publishing articles about the emperor from a very Japan-centered viewpoint, the reports in papers and magazines abroad looked at the emperor more broadly, from the perspective of outsiders. To the Japanese, these discussions were very harsh and took a totally unexpected position.

Ironically, the most extreme opinions appeared in the popular newspapers of England, the country that the Shōwa emperor most admired. These articles even stirred controversy between the two governments. Though the British comments are difficult for Japanese people to bear, they are an important part of the discourse, representing a segment of overseas opinion.*

On September 21, 1988, the British tabloid *The Sun* wrote:

> There are two reasons to be sorry about Emperor Hirohito being on his deathbed: 1) The fact that Hirohito lived this long, and 2) The fact that

*The following two quotations are from Asian People's Tribunal Organizing Committee, "Accounts of the Emperor in the Overseas Press" (Gaifūsha, 1988).

he will die without being punished for the most despicable crimes of this century.

In 1941, when the chiefs of the Japanese general staffs were planning crimes against the Western nations and their treacherous attack, Hirohito should have been able to make them suspend their plot by simply waving his hand. For the Japanese in those days, he was regarded as a god. But at that time, the emperor did nothing but compose meaningless poems.

When his savage soldiers killed and raped millions of defenseless Chinese, he did nothing. When thousands of Allied prisoners of war were brutalized and tortured, he did nothing. We in England still weep in sorrow for the 12,433 men and women who died in the Japanese prisoner of war camps.

While the Japanese forces marched toward victory, Hirohito spread his name and prestige as a great general throughout the world. Then, at the dawn of defeat, he abandoned the seat of "god" in order to save his worthless neck. He led Japan by his own hand to destruction and mass death by the atomic bombs. He has retained in the palm of his hand the sentiments of the superstitious and has easily deceived the Japanese people even to this day. [This quotation and the following one, translated from Japanese, approximate the original English wording.]

The article concludes, "When he dies, there will definitely be a special seat reserved for him in hell."

Another article, in the *Daily Star* of September 21, 1988, also caused anger in Japan. That article stated:

Just like Hitler, Hirohito believed that his people were of a superior race, and were destined to rule the world.

Hirohito's impossible dream was smashed to bits by the atomic bombs that brought down his blood-stained empire. But his arrogance was not crushed. In his radio broadcast announcing the downfall of Japan he refused to use the word *surrender.* Instead, he told people, "the circumstances of the war did not necessarily proceed favorably for us."

Though Hirohito is regarded by many people as a more sinister murderer than Hitler, he managed to escape retribution. However, the Allied Powers deprived him of all political authority, and among his own people several million have not forgiven him for plunging Japan into a massive state of chaos.

Hirohito has remained a leader in name only, far removed from the people while his nation has effected a remarkable recovery from its ruins. And yet even now the Japanese are ready to kneel down before him.

In contrast to the articles in the British tabloids, full of naked hostility, the daily South Korean newspaper *Tonga Ilbo* (East Asian Daily) published a truly dignified, thoughtful editorial in its January 9, 1989, issue. The critical editorial was based on a meticulous historical analysis of the era and contained a sharp warning to the Japanese government and people for not having formally apologized for Japan's brutal colonial administration and wartime actions. When this editorial in *Tonga Ilbo,* which represents the voice of the people of South Korea, is compared to Itō Takashi's article and to the others noted previously, one cannot help but feel that something important is lacking in the Japanese analysis. The Shōwa era definitely ended with the emperor's death, but this event did not signify a change in the history of Asia. The editorial in the *Tonga Ilbo* read:

> The death of Hirohito marks the end of the Shōwa era, the dark age of the twentieth century. It was a turbulent time in which the rise of imperialism, defeat, war and peace were all intertwined chaotically. In the middle of this whirlpool stood Hirohito. Before we send sentimental words of condolences, we must reflect upon the era that he led, and question the historical responsibility of the emperor system. The first half of the Shōwa era was a history of war and aggression. No matter how much he may try to deny it, the declaration of war was made in his name. Also, it is a grim reality that Japan's conquest of the Asian nations was made in the name of the emperor.
>
> In the midst of this dark typhoon we Koreans lost our lives, language, and names. Since childhood we were forced to memorize "the oath of imperial subjects," and were forced to endure the humiliation of military conscription, labor conscription, and service in defense units. . . . We cannot forget this even if we try.
>
> The scars left on our nation are still deep. Nonetheless, the emperor's wartime responsibility has not been stringently questioned. He merely expressed his "regrets" regarding the brutal policies imposed by the colonial administration. He did not express any formal apologies. This postwar conduct is different from that adopted by Germany and Italy.
>
> Of course, we must also note America's responsibility for making use of the emperor system as an instrument in its postwar control of Japan. However, even after the emperor had become "the symbol of the state and unity of the people," he still retained the right to appoint the prime minister and chief justice of the Supreme Court. Even after he removed

the veil of "a living god," and issued the rescript denying his divinity, a considerable number of Japanese still wish to uphold his status not only as the head of state but also as a god.

What is the significance of the "one hundred million people in a state of somber self-restraint," a so-called storm that swept across the Japanese islands when Hirohito became ill? The right-wing is even seeking to revise the constitution to make the emperor the head of the state again.

Even though Emperor Hirohito is now gone from this world, there are many reasons to reevaluate his wartime responsibility, as well as the crimes of colonial control. To do so sends a signal that the history of provocation, of war and colonial control, must not be repeated, and that the reemergence of imperialistic thought and nationalism must be controlled. We must keep a close watch over Japan's recent activities, and must be on our guard.

When the winds of unity between religion and government begin to blow in Japan, her neighbors begin to worry: there is a danger that the energy that congeals in the centripetal point that is the emperor will spread. The terrible result of such a development is clear from our history. The turn to imperialism and militarism is not simply a misfortune for Japan's neighbors, it is a misfortune for the Japanese themselves. The questions we raise now about past crimes has signficance from now into the future for Japan's neighbors as well as for the Japanese.*

Though the Korean daily raises the issue of "past crimes," Japan's commentators either deny them or deal with them skittishly. This gap is indeed great. The Shōwa era ended, swept away by the imposing state funeral rituals, without these important points being explored more deeply. But the responsibility still burdens Japan as other nations repeatedly point out.

*Reprinted in *Asahi Shinbun,* January 10, 1989.

Chapter 5

FACING THE
TWENTY-FIRST CENTURY

In looking back over the seven decades of the Shōwa era, from the 1920s to the end of the 1980s, it is hard to pick a single, most-important theme. During these years Japan's ambition to become a military superpower was crushed, its land was wasted by air raids, a miraculous postwar recovery took place, and it emerged as an economic superpower. Shōwa history is full of twists and turns. A closer look at the economic and cultural tides of these decades also reveals drastic change.

The 1920s and 30s were a transition period in many ways, from the economic prosperity of the First World War to the Great Depression, from the emergence of party government with the rise of Taishō democracy to democracy's quick collapse. These years saw the emergence of the struggle between the left and right, as the country sought a way out of the economic depression. Then the military rose to power and the entire nation rushed along the path of continental aggression. In the midst of these raging rapids, the Japanese people lost all hope for the future and were steeped in nihilistic despair. A large number of renowned songs were written and popularized during the 1930s with names like "Debune" ("Departing Ship"), "Kimi Koishi" ("Longing for You"), "Samurai Nippon" ("Samurai Japan"), "Sake wa Namida Ka Tameiki ka" ("Sake with Tears and Sighs"), "Kage o Shitaite" ("Following a Shadow"), "Namida no Watari-dori" ("Tears and the Flight of Migrating Birds"), and "Wakare no Buruzu" ("Farewell Blues").

The first half of the 1940s was a time of total war, and the second half was an era of destruction, defeat, and the recovery from starvation. The unprecedented occupation of Japan by a foreign army and the democratic reforms and total renewal of institutions under the occupation authorities required a major transformation in Japanese people's values. Again, the popular songs of the time clearly reflect the prevailing moods. In wartime, military songs like "Sora no Shimpei" ("The Divine Soldiers of the Sky") were, of course, ubiquitous. After the war came escapist tunes like "Naku na Kobato yo" ("Little Dove, Don't You Cry"), "Hoshi no Nagare" ("Drifting Stars"), and "Tokyo Bugi-Wugi" ("Tokyo Boogie Woogie").

In the 1950s, having overcome the worst of the war damages and recovered to prewar economic levels, Japan built a foundation for further economic growth. Hammers rang out the arrival of economic recovery, thanks to the U.S. military procurement contracts resulting from the war in Korea. Also at that time, public opinion split the political establishment over the peace treaty and the U.S.-Japan Mutual Security Pact. During this period, a wide range of traditional sentimental melodies—not to mention some foreign tunes—became hit songs. Among these were a song by Misora Hibari called "Ringo Oiwake" ("The Packhorse Driver's Apple Song") and "Que Será Será" and "The Banana Boat Song." This period also saw the rise of the movies as mass entertainment; some 504 commercial films were produced in 1958 alone.

The 1960s were the golden decade of high-speed economic growth, symbolized by high-profile international events like the Tokyo Olympiad in 1964 and the Osaka International Exposition at the end of the decade. In this period, the most drastic changes in lifestyle took place—what I have called the lifestyle revolution. It was the decade of the salaryman, the white-collar worker, and the air was filled with triumphant songs like "Ue o Muite Arukō" ("Let's Walk with Our Heads Up"), "Yume wa Yoru Hiraku" ("Dreams Blossom at Night"), "Bara ga Saita" ("The Roses Have Bloomed"), and "Sekai wa Futari no Tame ni" ("The World Is There for the Two of Us").

In the 1970s the Japanese economy adjusted itself in preparation for its second leap forward. In the latter half of the 1960s, Japan temporarily prolonged its economic growth thanks to Vietnam War procurements. But Vietnam War procurements ended in 1973, and in addition to student insurrections and lingering pollution problems, the country was hit by the oil shock. The high energy consumption of Japan's industrial system and the national tendencies toward mass production and mass consumption were called into question. A more individualistic, multifaceted society emerged in the 1970s; some called it the "age of fashion." But in song, people retreated to traditional tunes and images, with titles evoking pastoral scenes and bygone years, like "Kanda-gawa" ("The Kanda River"), "Shiku-ramen no Kaori" ("The Scent of Cyclamen"), "Oyoge, Taiyaki-kun" ("Swim, Little Sea Bream"), and "Tsugaru Kaikyo Fuyu Keshiki" ("Winter at the Tsugaru Straits").

The 1980s saw the rise of the information society and the proliferation of new kinds of crime. Following the Lockheed scandal, the Liberal

Democratic Party's brain trust embarked on the Recruit affair.* The cost of this affair was called the tab left by the seven-year reign of Prime Minister Nakasone Yasuhiro, sometimes referred to as Reagan's "younger brother." The value of the dollar fell, causing a surplus of money; land values and stocks skyrocketed, large gaps in wealth developed, and people's thinking became conservative. New singers appeared, popularizing such songs as "Yakiri no watashi" ("Fending off Arrows on the Ferry"), "Garasu no ringo" ("Apple in the Glass"), and "Sutaaraito" ("Starlight").

What Has Been Accomplished; What Remains to Be Done

After the war, the absolutist emperor system and military institutions that had enveloped Japan for almost eighty years since the Meiji Restoration were, to a certain extent, swept aside. I qualify this accomplishment because the political forces within the Diet capable of bringing about democratic changes in political authority still have not fully developed.

Indeed, because the hereditary position of the emperor and his special authority in the realm of state affairs have remained as symbols, a movement to restore the emperor as the head of state has emerged. The military, ostensibly banned under Chapter Two of the peace constitution, remains under the rubric of the so-called "self-defense forces" and is being strengthened. But these elements have remained under the civilian control of the Diet and the cabinet chosen by the people and, unlike the prewar years, are not functioning independently. However, civilian control in Japan is not firmly established and it could be overturned in the future. At present, the vast majority of the people support Article Nine of the constitution (see Appendix), which renounces war as a right of the state, and a period of respite continues.

The lifestyles of most Japanese improved enormously during the Shōwa era. Nearly the entire population has been freed from hunger, and most have decent housing, medical care, and education. Though many inadequacies still exist in housing conditions, community infrastructure, and social welfare, great improvements have been made since the war.

One major problem, however, has been largely ignored: the destruction of Japan's environment. Issues like the contamination of land by poi-

---

*In 1984 Recruit, a real estate firm, sold unlisted shares in their company to politicians and bureaucrats, enabling them to make huge profits when the stocks were traded over the counter. In return, Recruit got favorable government contracts.

sonous agricultural chemicals, waste from heavy industries, and radiation from nuclear powered electric plants must be dealt with much more urgently. Japan also must recognize the impact of its economy on other nations. Regions of the world where Japan gets it resources also are suffering the serious environmental consequences of Japan's development.

Based on the legacy of the Taishō democracy movement and the postwar democratic reforms, democracy as an institution has been established in Japan. But Japanese democracy is in danger as money politics continues to dominate the electoral process, resulting in scandal after scandal and eroding people's desire to participate. Fundamental reforms are needed. The forty-year rule of the Liberal Democratic Party produced systemic problems for Japanese democracy: corruption, political stagnation, irresponsible conduct, and loss of public confidence in politicians. To make a contribution to the world appropriate to its national strength, Japan first must institute political reforms by fundamentally restructuring the political parties.

Japanese foreign policy over the past eight decades has been very inconsistent. Before the war, the governments of prime ministers Shidehara, Konoe, and Matsuoka attempted to establish a firm policy, but governments and cabinets changed frequently in those years, and every new prime minister or foreign minister redirected Japan's foreign policy. Though it is impossible to characterize Japanese policy, some of the elder statesmen and advisers to the emperor urged cooperation with the United States and Great Britain and tried to control the forces pushing for a tripartite alliance with Germany and Italy. But the Konoe and Matsuoka cabinets adopted a hard-line, aggressive foreign policy not just toward China and the Soviet Union, but toward the United States and Britain as well, finally leading Japan to the all-or-nothing gamble of the Pacific War.

Compared to the prewar policies, the postwar years have an element of consistency: the foreign policy was simply to follow the United States. Japan had no genuine foreign policy. As a result, Japan was viewed in the international arena as an anonymous, faceless follower country—a country without an identity or a position. This impression was not simply a product of Japan's defeat and humiliation. Unlike Japan, West Germany engaged in stringent self-criticism for its war crimes, including the massacre of the Jews. Not only did the West German president voluntarily apologize for Germany's crimes, the dark history of these acts was taught and discussed throughout the national school system and the entire nation engaged in sincere self-reflection and penitence. Together with an active foreign aid program, this genuine soul-searching helped the Germans overcome their past and gain the respect of people throughout the world.

In contrast, Japan frequently became the object of protest, especially from neighboring nations, when the Japanese government attempted to whitewash the history of Japan's war crimes by rewriting history textbooks (Japan's attacks in China, for example, were called "advances") and obstructing efforts to teach the darker episodes of the war. The emperor and those who had been charged as class-A war criminals, like Kishi Nobusuke (who was Minister of Commerce and Industry at the time of Pearl Harbor and who became Prime Minister in 1957), refused to acknowledge Japan's acts of aggression or admit their responsiblity for these crimes. For this reason, some Koreans and Chinese still hold the Japanese in contempt as lacking moral principles. This attempt to cover up war crimes reveals a dark underside to the mindset of those Japanese who have meekly, quietly followed the United States.

In the area of discrimination and oppression, a certain amount of progress has been made, though there is much more to be done. Unfortunately, the progress has not been a result of specific government policies but, rather, resulted from the persistent demands and struggles of those below—including movements of the outcaste *burakumin* and the Korean-Japanese—to improve their social standing. But their struggles continue, and Japan still has serious problems with discrimination against women, the handicapped, and the Ainu and Okinawan populations.

In the case of women, discrimination is not just in the workplace, it is deeply embedded in the general consciousness. Though women are equal under the law, Japan remains a male-centered society. The feminist movement in Japan dates back to 1911, when Hiratsuka Raichō organized the *Seitōkai*, the Bluestocking Society, and published a journal for women aimed at helping them achieve independence. In those days, the feminist movement was seen as a struggle against the remains of the feudal patriarchal system. But by the 1960s—the age of the salaryman and the typical modern family of husband, wife, and two children—many women realized that sexism had not disappeared. On the contrary, they were firmly fastened to a modern patriarchal system that used the rationale of gender-differentiated social and professional roles to keep women out of many areas. Discrimination against women was not simply a feudal legacy.

The real indictment of modern sexism in Japan started with the feminist movement of 1970, the International Year of the Woman. A women's conference held in November of that year helped awaken Japanese women at all levels to begin pressing for more progress. Soon, common discriminatory practices like lower pay for equal work and forced early retirement were denounced as violations of the law. Existing laws on family registration (records on births, death, marriage, and so on held by local authorities) and divorce—laws that made it very difficult or impossible for women to control their lives—were reformed. Finally, in 1985, the Equal Employment Opportunity Law was passed, banning gender discrimination in the workplace.

Of course, Japan's long tradition of discrimination could not be suddenly reformed by a law, but the new awareness did become a lever that women could use to demand their right to equality in all segments of society. In September 1986, a woman, Doi Takako, became the chair of the Japan Socialist Party, then the leading opposition party. Doi's presence at the top of national politics inspired a "Doi boom" (a sharp rise in the number of female candidates) in the following national election, not necessarily because of Doi's achievements, but because women were able to take advantage of the rising tide of feminist awareness. How long will this trend continue as we move into the twenty-first century? The feminist transformation will be a movement to keep our eyes on.

When Iraqi dictator Saddam Hussein invaded Kuwait, setting off the Persian Gulf War, the coalition forces (mainly U.S. and British troops) drove back the Iraqis under the mandate of a United Nations Security Council resolution. This post-Cold War operation was seen by many as a milestone in world history, introducing a new era of harmony and cooperation. Indeed, Saddam Hussein is probably the last of his kind, an offspring of the Cold War superpowers who wove between the cracks of the Cold War conflict, purchased huge amounts of high-tech weapons, and waged a pointless war. But despite general international approval of the Gulf War, the key to world survival still is cooperation among potential rival nations and the resolution of international disputes by discussion.

The most significant development in global cooperation is the agreement issued by the Conference on Security and Cooperation in Europe (CSCE). The conference was organized when the unification of Germany prompted thirty-four of the world's wealthiest, most powerful nations (with a combined GNP of over sixty percent of the world total and about seventy percent of the world's military power), to conclude a treaty, known as the Paris Charter, to officially end the Cold War and move toward international cooperation and harmony.

One section of the Paris Charter, touching upon security guarantees, is almost exactly the same as the famous preamble to Japan's constitution. The Paris Charter states, "We recognize that it is a nation's indispensible duty to resolve disputes peacefully without the use or threat of force, that it is the fundamental ingredient for the preservation and strengthening of international peace and security." The similar statement in the Japanese constitution comes from Article Nine, which reads: "Aspiring sincerely to an international peace based on justice and order, the Japanese people forever renounce war as a sovereign right of the nation and the threat or use of force as a means of settling international disputes."

Ever since its adoption after the war, the Japanese constitution has been criticized harshly as being idealistic or impractical. Japan's postwar pacifism has subjected it to charges—from both inside and outside Japan—that it is without fundamental principles or ideals. With the acceptance of the Paris Charter, however, the principles outlined in Japan's constitution finally have won international recognition. From the beginning of the Cold War, the Japanese embraced the principle of peace, while it took forty-five years for other nations to catch on. Now, at last, there are massive arms limitation agreements among the former Cold War combatants. Japan, China, Russia, and South Korea should take the lead in spreading the tide of disarmament to Asia and developing organizations and concepts of friendship and cooperation to match the Paris Charter. If this ideal can spread into Asia, contentious issues such as the U.S.-Japan Mutual Security Pact and the reduction or elimination of the Japanese self-defense forces will be easier to resolve.

Japan has not attempted to spread the ideals it shares with the Paris Charter among Asian nations. Instead, Japan continues to identify with the West. Japanese leaders still constantly keep their eyes on the American mood and concentrate on following whatever the United States does. Now that the Cold War is over and Japan is an established economic power, Japan should make an international contribution worthy of its national strength by serving as a bridge to preserve peace between the Western nations and East Asia. If Japan plays such a role, as called for in its constitution, it finally will occupy the place of honor in the world that has eluded it so far.

The Emperor and the New Century

After Emperor Hirohito's death, Crown Prince Akihito, a product of the postwar years, ascended to the throne, but despite this generational transition, nothing really changed in the rituals and iconography of the succession. Akihito's ascent was carried out in more than ten ceremonies, the royal funeral, the ceremony of succession to the throne, the ceremony to inherit the imperial treasures, the ceremony of ascension to the throne, the grand ceremony of thanksgiving to the ancestral deities, and so on. All of these events followed the "tradition of the ancient ceremonies," which was formulated in the Meiji era when the emperor was first presented to the nation as a living deity.

The Shintō foundations of these ceremonies have been present since the Meiji era. Though controversy ensued when some citizens charged that state participation in these ceremonies violated the constitution, the government ignored the protests and the ceremonies were elaborately staged as state functions. The ceremonies were presented on television as fantasy-like, beautiful performances, capturing the hearts of the young generation. Thus, the emperor system under the new emperor is secure, even though Emperor Akihito lacks his father's charisma.

The atmosphere surrounding the imperial court is still highly conservative and little has changed, even with the arrival of the new Heisei era. The Ministry of Education continues to require schools to unfurl the Japanese flag and have students sing the national anthem (actions seen by many as imperial symbols of wartime spirit) on special occasions. Yasukuni Shrine (where the spirits of the war dead are said to dwell) and its military museum are still given official blessing. The chrysanthemum taboo restricting freedom of speech about the imperial family is also strong, as the murder of an *Asahi Shinbun* reporter, the shooting of Mayor Motoshima of Nagasaki, and other acts of intimidation and terror continue to inhibit open discussion.

What lies ahead for Japan's imperial court in the next century? The emperor system always has changed with the times and undoubtedly will continue to do so. But in the twenty-first century, Japan needs an emperor who can be a completely free person in society. The emperor should no longer be the symbol of the state and unity of the people, and succession to throne should not be hereditary. The emperor also should be relieved of the government functions assigned to him in the constitution, such as his attestation of the appointment and dismissal of ministers of state and judges of the state courts; his attestation of general and special amnesty, commutation of punishment, and reprieve; and his duty to award honors, receive foreign ambassadors and ministers, and perform ceremonial functions. The Japanese people should guarantee the emperor and the royal family the ability to live freely as normal citizens with human rights.

These measures would require changes in the constitution. Article One, for example, should simply state, "The sovereign authority in the Japanese nation resides with the people," and the responsibilities set out in Articles Two through Eight should be reassigned to the prime minister.

This denial of the emperor system must not be equated with denial of the imperial family's significance. I have studied Japanese history for many years and deeply appreciate the significance of the emperor and imperial court in our history. In particular, they have played a vital role in the preservation and continuation of Japan's cultural heritage. Japan abounds with historical landmarks, shrines, temples, and other cultural artifacts that express the profound relationship between the imperial court and Japanese culture. After all, this relationship has continued for 1,500 years.

Yet I do not defend the emperor system—as these pages have indicated, I am a critic. The imperial court, with its historical significance, has an appropriate place in a truly modern Japan. The emperor and his family should leave their sequestered, remote life in the castle in Toyko, which was the seat of the Tokugawa shoguns for generations, and return to the Kyoto imperial palace, the home of Japan's emperors for a thousand years. As far as I know, this was the Meiji emperor's lifelong desire. I would like to see the emperor return to his home community and enjoy the life of a free citizen.

If the imperial family abandoned their special privileges, the emperor, as a person interested in culture, could work quietly for the preservation of traditional art and Japanese culture. Just as there are high-level masters in Nō, flower arrangement, and the tea ceremony, the emperor could become the master of traditional Japanese culture and make the historical role of the imperial line come to life. The people of Japan would most likely greatly appreciate an emperor following this kind of lifestyle. Could it be that the members of the imperial court also desire this lifestyle, from the bottom of their hearts? In any case, no one should be able to take advantage of the emperor and the imperial court in any manner for any reason. As one who has lived through the entire painful history of the Shōwa era, this is my sincere hope.

EXCERPT FROM THE CONSTITUTION OF JAPAN

We, the Japanese people, acting through our duly elected representatives in the National Diet, determined that we shall secure for ourselves and our posterity the fruits of peaceful cooperation with all nations and the blessings of liberty throughout this land, and resolved that never again shall we be visited with the horrors of war through the action of government, do proclaim that sovereign power resides with the people and do firmly establish this Constitution. Government is a sacred trust of the people, the authority for which is derived from the people, the powers of which are exercised by the representatives of the people, and the benefits of which are enjoyed by the people. This is a universal principle of mankind upon which this Constitution is founded. We reject and revoke all constitutions, laws, ordinances, and rescripts in conflict herewith.

We, the Japanese people, desire peace for all time and are deeply conscious of the high ideals controlling human relationship, and we have determined to preserve our security and existence, trusting in the justice and faith of the peace-loving peoples of the world. We desire to occupy an honored place in an international society striving for the preservation of peace, and the banishment of tyranny and slavery, oppression and intolerance for all time from the earth. We recognize that all peoples of the world have the right to live in peace, free from fear and want.

We believe that no nation is responsible to itself alone, but that laws of political morality are universal; and that obedience to such laws is incumbent upon all nations who would sustain their own sovereignty and justify their sovereign relationship with other nations.

We, the Japanese people, pledge our national honor to accomplish these high ideals and purposes with all our resources.

CHAPTER I. *The Emperor*

ARTICLE 1. The Emperor shall be the symbol of the State and of the unity of the people, deriving his position from the will of the people with whom resides sovereign power.

ARTICLE 2. The Imperial Throne shall be dynastic and succeeded to in accordance with the Imperial House Law passed by the Diet.

ARTICLE 3. The advice and approval of the Cabinet shall be required for all acts of the Emperor in matters of state, and the Cabinet shall be responsible therefor.

ARTICLE 4. The Emperor shall perform only such acts in matters of state as are provided for in this Constitution and he shall not have powers related to government.

2. The Emperor may delegate the performance of his acts in matters of state as may be provided by law.

ARTICLE 5. When, in accordance with the Imperial House Law, a Regency is established, the Regent shall perform his acts in matters of state in the Emperor's name. In this case, paragraph one of the preceding article will be applicable.

ARTICLE 6. The Emperor shall appoint the Prime Minister as designated by the Diet.

2. The Emperor shall appoint the Chief Judge of the Supreme Court as designated by the Cabinet.

ARTICLE 7. The Emperor, with the advice and approval of the Cabinet, shall perform the following acts in matters of state on behalf of the people:

(1) Promulgation of amendments of the constitution, laws, cabinet orders and treaties;

(2) Convocation of the Diet;

(3) Dissolution of the House of Representatives;

(4) Proclamation of general election of members of the Diet;

(5) Attestation of the appointment and dismissal of Ministers of State and other officials as provided for by law, and of full powers and credentials of Ambassadors and Ministers;

(6) Attestation of general and special amnesty, commutation of punishment, reprieve, and restoration of rights;

(7) Awarding of honors;

(8) Attestation of instruments of ratification and other diplomatic documents as provided for by law;

(9) Receiving foreign ambassadors and ministers;

(10) Performance of ceremonial functions.

ARTICLE 8. No property can be given to, or received by, the Imperial House, nor can any gifts be made therefrom, without the authorization of the Diet.

CHAPTER II. *Renunciation of War*

ARTICLE 9. Aspiring sincerely to an international peace based on justice and order, the Japanese people forever renounce war as a sovereign right of the nation and the threat or use of force as means of settling international disputes.
2. In order to accomplish the aim of the preceding paragraph, land, sea, and air forces, as well as other war potential, will never be maintained. The right of belligerency of the state will not be recognized.

CHAPTER III. *Rights and Duties of the People*

ARTICLE 10. The conditions necessary for being a Japanese national shall be determined by law.

ARTICLE 11. The people shall not be prevented from enjoying any of the fundamental human rights. These fundamental human rights guaranteed to the people by this Constitution shall be conferred upon the people of this and future generations as eternal and inviolate rights.

ARTICLE 12. The freedoms and rights guaranteed to the people by this Constitution shall be maintained by the constant endeavor of the people, who shall refrain from any abuse of these freedoms and rights and shall always be responsible for utilizing them for the public welfare.

ARTICLE 13. All of the people shall be respected as individuals. Their right to life, liberty, and the pursuit of happiness shall, to the extent that it does not interfere with the public welfare, be the supreme consideration in legislation and in other governmental affairs.

ARTICLE 14. All of the people are equal under the law and there shall be no discrimination in political, economic or social relations because of race, creed, sex, social status or family origin.
2. Peers and peerage shall not be recognized.
3. No privilege shall accompany any award of honor, decoration or any distinction, nor shall any such award be valid beyond the lifetime of the individual who now holds or hereafter may receive it.

ARTICLE 15. The people have the inalienable right to choose their public officials and to dismiss them.
2. All public officials are servants of the whole community and not of any group thereof.
3. Universal adult suffrage is guaranteed with regard to the election of public officials.
4. In all elections, secrecy of the ballot shall not be violated. A voter shall not be answerable, publicly or privately, for the choice he has made.

ARTICLE 16. Every person shall have the right of peaceful petition for the redress of damage, for the removal of public officials, for the enactment, repeal or amendment of laws, ordinances or regulations and for other matters, nor shall any person be in any way discriminated against for sponsoring such a petition.

ARTICLE 17. Every person may sue for redress as provided by law from the State or a public entity, in case he has suffered damage through illegal act of any public official.

ARTICLE 18. No person shall be held in bondage of any kind. Involuntary servitude, except as punishment for crime, is prohibited.

ARTICLE 19. Freedom of thought and conscience shall not be violated.

ARTICLE 20. Freedom of religion is guaranteed to all. No religious organization shall receive any privileges from the State nor exercise any political authority.

2. No person shall be compelled to take part in any religious act, celebration, rite or practice.

3. The State and its organs shall refrain from religious education or any other religious activity.

ARTICLE 21. Freedom of assembly and association as well as speech, press and all other forms of expression are guaranteed.

2. No censorship shall be maintained, nor shall the secrecy of any means of communication be violated.

ARTICLE 22. Every person shall have freedom to choose and change his residence and to choose his occupation to the extend that it does not interfere with the public welfare.

2. Freedom of all persons to move to a foreign country and to divest themselves of their nationality shall be inviolate.

ARTICLE 23. Academic freedom is guaranteed.

ARTICLE 24. Marriage shall be based only on the mutual consent of both sexes and it shall be maintained through mutual cooperation with the equal rights of husband and wife as a basis.

2. With regard to choice of spouse, property rights, inheritance, choice of domicile, divorce and other matters pertaining to marriage and the family, laws shall be enacted from the standpoint of individual dignity and the essential equality of the sexes.

ARTICLE 25. All people shall have the right to maintain the minimum standards of wholesome and cultured living.

2. In all spheres of life, the State shall use its endeavors for the promotion and extension of social welfare and security, and of public health.

ARTICLE 26. All people shall have the right to receive an equal education correspondent to their ability, as provided by law.

2. All people shall be obligated to have all boys and girls under their protection receive ordinary education as provided for by law. Such compulsory education shall be free.

ARTICLE 27. All people shall have the right and the obligation to work.

2. Standards for wages, hours, rest and other working conditions shall be fixed by law.

3. Children shall not be exploited.

ARTICLE 28. The right of workers to organize and to bargain and act collectively is guaranteed.

ARTICLE 29. The right to own or to hold property is inviolable.

2. Property rights shall be defined by law, in conformity with the public welfare.

3. Private property may be taken for public use upon just compensation therefor.

ARTICLE 30. The people shall be liable to taxation as provided by law.

ARTICLE 31. No person shall be deprived of life or liberty, nor shall any other criminal penalty be imposed, except according to procedure established by law.

ARTICLE 32. No person shall be denied the right of access to the courts.

ARTICLE 33. No person shall be apprehended except upon warrant issued by a competent judicial officer which specifies the offense with which the person is charged, unless he is apprehended, the offense being committed.

ARTICLE 34. No person shall be arrested or detained without being at once informed of the charges against him or without the immediate privilege of counsel; nor shall he be detained without adequate cause; and upon demand of any person such cause must be immediately shown in open court in his presence and the presence of his counsel.

ARTICLE 35. The right of all persons to be secure in their homes, papers and effects against entries, searches and seizures shall not be impaired except upon warrant issued for adequate cause and particularly describing the place to be searched and things to be seized, or except as provided by Article 33.

2. Each search or seizure shall be made upon separate warrant issued by a competent judicial officer.

ARTICLE 36. The infliction of torture by any public officer and cruel punishments are absolutely forbidden.

ARTICLE 37. In all criminal cases the accused shall enjoy the right to a speedy and public trial by an impartial tribunal.

2. He shall be permitted full opportunity to examine all witnesses, and he shall have the right of compulsory process for obtaining witnesses on his behalf at public expense.

3. At all times the accused shall have the assistance of competent counsel who shall, if the accused is unable to secure the same by his own efforts, be assigned to his use by the State.

ARTICLE 38. No person shall be compelled to testify against himself.

2. Confession made under compulsion, torture or threat, or after prolonged arrest or detention shall not be admitted in evidence.

3. No person shall be convicted or punished in cases where the only proof against him is his own confession.

ARTICLE 39. No person shall be held criminally liable for an act which was lawful at the time it was committed, or of which he has been acquitted, nor shall he be placed in double jeopardy.

ARTICLE 40. Any person, in case he is acquitted after he has been arrested or detained, may sue the State for redress as provided by law.

CHAPTER IV. *The Diet*

ARTICLE 41. The Diet shall be the highest organ of state power, and shall be the sole law-making organ of the State.

ARTICLE 42. The Diet shall consist of two Houses, namely the House of Representatives and the House of Councillors.

ARTICLE 43. Both Houses shall consist of elected members, representative of all the people.

2. The number of the members of each House shall be fixed by law.

ARTICLE 44. The qualifications of members of both Houses and their electors shall be fixed by law. However, there shall be no discrimination because of race, creed, sex, social status, family origin, education, property or income.

ARTICLE 45. The term of office of members of the House of Representatives shall be four years. However, the term shall be terminated before the full term is up in case the House of Representatives is dissolved.

ARTICLE 46. The term of office of members of the House of Councillors shall be six years, and election for half the members shall take place every three years.

ARTICLE 47. Electoral districts, method of voting and other matters pertaining to the method of election of members of both Houses shall be fixed by law.

ARTICLE 48. No person shall be permitted to be a member of both Houses simultaneously.

ARTICLE 49. Members of both Houses shall receive appropriate annual payment from the national treasury in accordance with law.

ARTICLE 50. Except in cases provided by law, members of both Houses shall be exempt from apprehension while the Diet is in session, and any members apprehended before the opening of the session shall be freed during the term of the session upon demand of the House.

ARTICLE 51. Members of both Houses shall not be held liable outside the House for speeches, debates or votes cast inside the House.

INDEX

Abé Nobuyuki, 89
Abe Sada affair, 19
Air raids, 30, 32, 33, 34–35,
    44–45, 46
Akihito, 11, 95, 99, 104, 108, 109,
    110, 111, 124, 126, 145
Akishino, Prince, 124
Akutagawa Ryūnosuke, 10, 10n
Amaterasu Omikami, 34, 40, 127
America. *See* United States
American culture in Japan, 6–7, 18
Anti-Japanese People's United
    Front, 21, 22
Araki, General, 84
Arms limitations treaties, 11, 14, 74
Army. *See* Military
Asano Akira, 17
Atomic bombings, 30, 33, 93, 114
Automobile industry, 51, 52, 57,
    59, 60
Awaya Kentaro, 79
Aya, Prince, 110

Bantō Kazutoshi, 30, 31
Baseball, 18
Bergamini, David, 93
Berlin Olympics, 19
Biotechnology, 58
Bluestocking Society, 142

Britain. *See* Great Britain
Bullet trains, 53, 59, 109
Burakumin (outcasts), 111, 121,
    142

Cabinet ministers, 81, 86–87
Canon, 54
Carter, Jimmy, 114
Censorship, 19, 24–25, 38, 110,
    111, 115, 145
Chemical industries, 41, 44, 45,
    46, 52
Chiang Kai-shek, 21
Chichibu, Prince, 73
China: contempt for Japanese, 142;
    Japanese attack on Nanjing, 28;
    Japanese occupation of Shan-
    dong Province in, 28, 74;
    Japan's war with, 3, 19, 20–21,
    22, 42, 115, 126; Jinan Incident,
    74–75; and Manchurian Inci-
    dent, 11, 12, 13, 15, 22, 28,
    75–78, 85; population of, 22;
    revolution in, 37–38; and
    Shanghai Incident, 18, 78–80;
    and Spanish Civil War, 19; Xian
    Incident, 21–23
Chokunin (direct imperial ap-
    pointees), 120–21

153

Chrysanthemum taboo, 110, 111, 115, 145

Cinema. *See* Movies

Clothing, 26, 42, 51–52, 60

Coal production, 50, 55

Communist Party, 15–17, 23, 38, 101, 103, 105

Computers, 58, 59, 65

Conference on Security and Cooperation in Europe (CSCE), 143–44

Constitutions: excerpt from postwar constitution, 147–52; Meiji Constitution, 75–76, 81, 120–21, 128–29; new postwar constitution, 106–107, 144, 145–52; suggested changes in postwar constitution, 145–46

Consumerism, 59–60, 111

Control faction, 84

Cooperative Finance Commission, 51

Counter-culture movement, 55–56

Crime, 66–70, 139–40

Daijin (heads of government ministries), 112

Daimyō (lords), 120

Deaths: annual death rates, 2–3; from pollution, 62; in Sino-Japanese War, 3; from starvation and malnutrition following World War II, 37; from traffic accidents, 3; in World War II, 29, 30

Defense industries, 42–43, 44, 46

Deng Xiaoping, 114

Depression. *See* Great Depression

Diseases. *See* Illnesses

Dodge, Joseph, 49

Dodge line, 49

Doi boom, 143

Doi Takako, 143

Dyke, Col. Kenneth, 101–102, 105

Earthquake, 6, 7, 9, 74

East Asian Anti-Japanese Remilitarization front, 66–67

Eastern Europe, 59

Economy: automobile industry, 51; dollar-yen ratio, 57; doubts about economic growth, 55–56; export trade, 57–58; GNP, 62, 117; in Great Depression, 7–9, 12–15; high- speed economic growth, in 1950s-1960s, 40–41, 52–59, 62–63, 108–109, 117, 139; and household incomes, 60, 61; industrial and chemical manufacturing in 1930s, 41, 44, 45; inflation, 44–45, 49, 58; and information technology, 58; Iwato boom, 40, 60, 108, 109; Izanagi boom, 40, 54–55, 60; and Korean War procurements, 51; labor productivity, 62; munitions plants in 1930s, 42–43, 44; and National Mobilization Law, 24–25, 42–43; in 1973-1985, 56–57, 140–41; from 1985-1990, 57–58, 140–41; and occupation reforms, 38–39, 43, 46–49; oil crisis and recovery, 56–59; postwar recovery, 49–52; recovery of, in mid-to-late 1930s, 18, 41; Shoup tax system, 49–51; stock market drop in 1989, 58–59; and Vietnam War procurements, 51, 53–54, 139; wartime economic system, 40–45; *zaibatsu* (family-based conglomerates), 13, 38, 41, 46–47, 87

Education, 38–39, 48, 68, 145

Electrical appliance industry, 51, 52, 60

Electrical power, 50

Elizabeth, Queen, 110, 111, 113, 114

Emperor system: and abandoned soldiers, 118–20; and ceremonies at Akihito's ascent, 145; changes in, 122–24, 145–46; and declaration of being human, 126–29; and emperor as god, 34, 82, 117, 126–27; and emperor's views of people, 124–25; external structure of, 120–21, 122; and national polity, 125–26; organ theory of, 84–85, 86, 128; and popular nationalism, 116–18; and suppression of information, 24–25; underside of, 121–22

England. *See* Great Britain

Enka music, 66

Environmental pollution. *See* Pollution

Equal Employment Opportunity Law, 60, 143

Ethiopia, Italian invasion of, 19

Export trade, 57–58

Expressways, 53, 109

Factory work. *See* Manufacturing

Far East International Military Tribunal, 28–29, 104. *See also* War crimes trials in Tokyo

Farmers, 7–8, 38, 41, 43, 45, 55, 62

February 26 Incident, 14, 15, 19

Federation of Economic Organizations (Keidanren), 61

Feminist movement, 55, 142–43

Feng, Prime Minister, 114

Films. *See* Movies

Fishermen, 62

Food: enjoyment of, 60; increased food production after World War II, 51; rationing of, during World War II, 25–27, 42; shortages of, after World War II, 37, 46–47, 50, 102

Ford, Gerald, 114

Foreign Ministry, 112

Foreign policy, 113–14, 141–42. *See also* specific countries

France, 20, 28, 113

Franco, Francisco, 19, 20

Fujiya Confectionary Corporation, 68

Fukazawa Shichirō, 116

Futabayama, 19

Geisha, 8

General Headquarters of Allied Powers. *See* GHQ (General Headquarters of Allied Powers)

Germany. *See* Nazi Germany; West Germany

GHQ (General Headquarters of Allied Powers): establishment of, 36; and Hirohito's national tour, 101–102, 105, 106; and Okinawa occupation, 99–101, 106; and postwar recovery, 50; reforms imposed by, 38–39, 43

GNP, 62, 117

Godaigo, 71

Great Britain: and arms limitations treaties, 11, 14; evaluation of Hirohito by newspapers in, 134–36; Hirohito's visit to, 113; Japanese declaration of war against, 87–92; and Persian Gulf War, 143; and Spanish Civil War, 20; in World War II, 28

Great Depression, 7–9, 12–15, 41, 138

Great Japanese Industrial Patriotic Association, 22

Great Kantō Earthquake, 6, 7, 9, 74

Gunther, John, 124–25

Hani Motoko, 7

Hannin (junior appointees), 121

Hanpei (palace guard), 120

Hara Kei, 73, 74

Hata Shunroku, 86, 87

Hayashi Senjūrō, 11, 77, 78, 89

Higashikuni Moriatsu, Prince, 36, 38, 44

Hiranuma Kiichirō, 27, 31–32, 89

Hiratsuka Raicho, 142

Hiro, Prince, 110

Hirohito: and abandoned soldiers after World War II, 118–20; and abdication, 98–99; arrogation of authority of, by army, 77–80; assassination attempt on, 9–10, 74; beginnings of reign of, 10–11, 74–77; birth of, 72; British evaluation of, 134–36; and cabinet makeup, 86–87, 88; as constitutional monarch, 13–15, 80–84, 128–29, 130–31; death of, 116, 129–30; and declaration of being human, 126–29; and declaration of war against America and England, 87–92, 95–96, 141; education of, 72–74; European tour of, 110, 113; and foreign policy, 113–14; as god, 34, 82, 117, 126–27; as head of state, 112–13; illness of, 110, 115–16, 122, 123, 124, 129; and imperial family, 109–11; Japan tour by, 101–107, 108; Japanese intellectuals' evaluation of, 130–34; Korean evaluation of, 136–37; length of reign of, 71; lifestyle as young man before becoming emperor, 9; and MacArthur, 94–95, 97, 99, 105–106, 124–25; media coverage of, 109–11, 114, 115–16, 129–30; myths and folklore about, 82, 97–98, 126; name at birth, 72; and new constitution, 108–16, 148; and occupation, 99–107; and Okinawa occupation, 99–101, 106; poetry of, 79, 96, 97; public opinion on, 103–105, 123–24, 125; as regent, 9, 74, 75, 82; and responsibility for inaction, 85–86, 90; and responsibility for World War II, 130–37, 142; significance of, 71; Soliloquy of, 30–33, 44, 91–92, 94, 95–96, 125–26, 133; statement of, calling for negotiated peace, 30–33, 44, 93–94, 125–26; supreme authority of, before and during World War II, 80–87, 90, 120–21, 128–29; and Tōjō Hideki, 82–83; U.S. visit by,

110, 113–14; views of people,
124–25; and war crimes trials,
80, 85, 101; and weakening of
constitutional government in
1930s, 13–15, 83–86, 128–29;
and World War II, 30–35
Hiroshima, 30, 93
Hirota Kōki, 32–33, 84, 89
Hitachi, 52, 54
Hitler, Adolf, 12, 14, 19, 20, 27,
32, 84, 135
Honda, 47, 54
Honjō Shigeru, 77, 78
Hosokawa Morisada, 93
Housing, 60–61, 140
Hull, Cordell, 88
Human rights: constitutional pro-
tection of, 149–52; violations
before World War II, 10, 15–18,
25, 103, 131–32
Hussein, Saddam, 143

Ikeda Hayato, 49
Illnesses, 37, 55–56, 116–17
Imperial Household Agency, 111,
115
Imperial Rescript to Soldiers and
Sailors, 83, 84, 133
Imperial Rule Assistance Associa-
tion, 22, 133
Imperial Way faction, 84
Income, 60, 61
Industries. *See* Manufacturing
Inflation, 44–45, 49, 58
Information revolution, 58, 59,
62–63, 64–66
Information, suppression of, 19,
24–25
International Monetary Fund, 53
International Year of the Woman,

143
Inukai Tsuyoshi, 11, 14, 83, 84,
132
Iriye Sukemasa, 100, 104, 106,
107
Ishikawa Tatsuzō, 7
Ishimure Michiko, 116
Ishiwara Kanji, 11, 22, 77, 78
Ishizaka Taizō, 61
Isogai Rensuke, 86–87
Itagaki Seishirō, 85, 86
Italy, 19, 22, 85–86
Itō Chiyoko, 17
Itō Noe, 10
Itō Takashi, 31, 130–31
Iwato boom, 40, 60, 108, 109
Izanagi boom, 40, 54–55, 60

Japan Nitrogen Fertilizer Company
(Chisso), 46, 50, 87
Japan Socialist Party, 54, 143
Japan-U.S. Mutual Security Pact,
52, 108, 109, 110, 130, 139,
144
Japanese-German Anti-Comintern
Pact, 19
Japanese International Exposition
Association, 61
Jazz, 18
Jinan Incident, 74–75
Jiyū Gakuen (Free School), 7
Jizō, 64
Journals. *See* Magazines and jour-
nals

Kan'in, Prince, 79, 85
Kannon, 64
Karaoke machines, 65–66
Kataribe (storytellers), 65
Katō Tomosaburō, 74

Kawabe Torajiro, 31
Kawakami Hajime, 15–16
Kawamura Sumiyoshi, 72
Kawasaki, 46
Kaya, Prince, 83
Keenan, Joseph B., 80, 100, 101
Keidanren (Federation of Economic Organizations), 61
Kellogg-Briand international peace pact, 28–29
Kenmu Restoration, 71
Kennan, George, 100
Khrushchev, Nikita, 20
Kido Kōichi, 72, 79–80, 85, 90, 94, 133
Kido Takamasa, 72
Kikutake Rokkō, 24
Kinoshita Michio, 94, 95, 97, 102, 107, 127
Kiryū Yūyū, 24
Kobayashi Takiji, 16, 17, 17n
Kohoe Fumimaro, Prince, 22
Koizumi, Shinzō, 111
Kojima Noburu, 89
Kokutai (national polity), 18, 25, 94, 125–26
Kōmoto Daisaku, Col., 75–77
Konoe Fumimaro, 14, 32, 33, 34, 84, 89, 93, 141
Korea, 41, 77, 136–37, 142
Korean War, 51–52
Kōzaha Faction, 120
Kozuka Kinshichi, 119
Kuninomiya Nagako, Princess, 10
Kuwait, 143
Kuyoura Keigo, 10
Kwantung Army, 11, 13, 75, 77, 78

Labor productivity, 62
Labor unions, 38, 42, 48, 57
Land reform, 38, 43, 46, 47–48
Land speculation, 58
LDP. See Liberal Democratic Party (LDP)
League of Nations: Japan's withdrawal from, 11–12, 14; Lytton Commission of, 78
Liberal Democratic Party (LDP), 50, 139–40, 141
Lifestyle revolution. See Urban culture
Lockheed scandal, 139
Lytton Commission, 78

MacArthur, Gen. Douglas, 2, 35–36, 49, 94–95, 97, 99, 105–106, 124–25, 127
Magazines and journals, 7, 24, 110, 142
Maids, 8
Makino Nobuaki, 78
Malik, Yakov, 32–33
Manchuria, 11, 13, 28, 30, 33, 41, 77–78, 79, 85
Manchurian Incident, 11, 12, 13, 15, 22, 28, 75–78, 85
Manufacturing: automobile industry, 51, 52, 57, 59, 60; electrical appliance industry, 51, 52, 60; industrial and chemical manufacturing in 1930s, 41, 44, 45, 46, 52; munitions plants in 1930s, 42–43, 44, 46; steel industry, 52; women's employment as factory workers, 6, 8
Marshall, George C., 99
Masaki Hiroshi, 24

Mass media. *See* Newspapers; Television

Matsuda Yūsaku, 69

Matsudaira Keimin, 95

Matsudaira Yasumasa, 95

Matsuoka, Prime Minister, 141

Matsushita, 52, 54

May 15th Incident, 11, 14, 83, 132

Media. *See* Newspapers; Television

Meiji Constitution, 75–76, 81, 120–21, 128–29

Meiji emperor, 71, 72, 93

Meiji Restoration, 5, 71, 120, 140

Meyerhold, V. Y., 24

Michiko, Princess, 108, 109, 110

Microelectronics, 58

Mikasa, Prince, 9

Military: abandoned soldiers after World War II, 118–20; arrogation of emperor's authority by, 77–80; civilian control of, 140; control faction of army, 84; coups planned by, in 1930s, 14–15; Hirohito as supreme commander of, 80–86; Imperial Rescript to Soldiers and Sailors, 83, 84, 133; Imperial Way faction in army, 84; and London naval arms limitations treaty, 11; and Manchurian Incident, 11, 12, 13, 75–77; and May 15th Incident, 11, 14, 83; response of, to Great Depression, 12–15

Miller, Mariko Terasaki, 30, 94, 95

Minakata Kumakusu, 73

Minamata disease, 55, 61, 62, 116–117

Ministry of Agriculture and Forestry, 43

Minobe Tatsukichi, 84, 128

Minseitō party, 22

Mishima Yukio, 124

Mitsubishi, 41, 46, 47, 54, 67–68

Mitsui, 41, 46, 47

Miyamoto Kenji, 38

Miyazawa Kenji, 8

Miyoshi Tatsuji, 104

M-kun, 66, 69–70

Mori Ōgai, 73

Mori (Shōwa Electric), 46

Morinaga Corporation, 67, 68

Morinaga Powdered Milk Incident, 68

Motoshima Hitoshi, 116, 145

Movies, 6, 7, 18, 69, 116–17, 139

Munitions plants. *See* Defense industries

Music, 18, 55, 65–66, 138–40

Mutshuito, 9n

Nabeyama Sadachika, 16

Nagasaki, 30, 93

Nakamura Teruo, 119–20

Nakano Yoshio, 103–104

Nakasone Yasuhiro, 98, 111, 112, 140

Namba Taisuke, 74

Nanba Taisuke, 10

Nashimoto, Prince, 94

National brand, 52

National Landowners' Association, 47

National Mobilization Law, 25–26, 42–43

National polity (*kokutai*), 18, 25, 94, 125–26

Navy. *See* Military

Nazi Germany: expansion into neighboring countries, 12, 14; military successes during World War II, 27–28; and Nazi-Soviet pact, 27; rise of, 11–12; and Spanish Civil War, 19–20; and Stalin, 20; surrender of, in World War II, 32; in Tripartite Alliance, 22, 85–86

New Deal, 12

Newspapers, 24, 109–11, 115–16, 123, 129–37

Nissan, 46, 54, 87

Nitobe Inazō, 73

Nittoku Metal Industries, 54

Nixon, Richard, 57

Nogi Maresuke, Gen., 72

Noro Eitarō, 16

Nosaka Sanzō, 103

Nozaka Akiyuki, 37

Occupation: GHQ established during, 36; and Hirohito, 99–107; Hirohito's national tour during, 101–102, 105, 106; illness and malnutrition during, 37, 45–46; and MacArthur, 35–36; Okinawa occupation, 99–101, 106; reforms during, 38–39, 43, 46–49

Ogawa Heikichi, 76

Oikawa, Admiral, 88, 91

Oil industry, 56–57, 58

Okada Keisuke, 89

Okada Yoshiko, 23–24

Okinawa, Battle of, 91–92, 100

Okinawa occupation, 99–101, 106

Olympic games, 19, 53, 109, 139

Onoda Hiroo, 119

Organ theory, 84–85, 86, 128

Organization for Economic Cooperation and Development, 53

Osaka International Exposition, 61, 109, 112, 139

Osugi Sakae, 10

Panasonic brand, 52

Paris Charter, 144

Patriotic Women's Association, 26

Peace Preservation Law, 10, 15–18, 25, 38, 103, 122, 131–32

Persian Gulf War, 143

Philippines, 29, 30, 91–92

Pollution, 55, 61–62, 116–17, 140–41

Potsdam Declaration, 33, 37, 93, 99, 100, 125

Poverty, 7–9, 37, 55, 62

Prime ministers, selection of, 83–84

Prostitution, 8, 37

Radio, 18–19, 24, 115

Recruit affair, 140, 140n

Riken, 46

Rites of passage, 63–64

Robot technology, 58

Sackett, Henry A., 79, 80, 85

Saionji Kinmochi, 73, 75, 76, 78, 84, 86

Sakanoue Yuki, 116–18

Sakomizu Hisatsune, 33

San Francisco Peace Treaty, 104, 107

Sano Manabu, 16

Sanyo, 52

Sato Eisaku, 54, 61

Satō Kenryō, 82

Scandals, 19, 139–40

Sebald, William J., 99, 101, 106
Seitōkai (Bluestocking Society),
   142
Seiyūkai party, 22, 75
Sewing machines, 52
Sexism, 60, 142–43
Sexual discrimination, 60
Sexuality, 60
Shandong Province, 28, 74
Shanghai Incident, 18, 78–80
Sharp, 52
Shidehara Kijūrō, 74, 75, 87,
   126–27, 141
Shimomura Kainan, 94
Shindō Eiichi, 99, 100
Shirai, Jack, 20
Shirakawa, General, 78–79
Shirakawa Tama, 79
Shōda Michiko, 108
Shoup, Carl S., 49
Shoup tax system, 49–51
Shōwa Electric Industry, 46, 50, 87
Shōwa era: beginning of, 10–11;
   emperor's records of, 2; end of,
   129–37; lenth of, 2, 5, 10;
   meaning of name, 9n. *See also*
   Hirohito
Sino-Japanese War. *See* China
Smith, Adam, 54
SMON (subacute myelo-
   opticoneuropathy), 55–56
Social Mass Party (Shakai
   Taishūtō), 42
Socialist Party, 54, 143
Sōnin (appointees with imperial
   sanction), 120–21
Sonoda Sunao, 117
Sony, 47, 52, 54
Soviet Union: clash with Japanese
   army at Changgufeng, 85; Great

Purge in, 23–24; Japanese defec-
   tors to, 23–24; Japanese intel-
   lectuals' views on, 20; Japanese
   policy toward, in 1945, 32–33;
   Nazi invasion of, 28; and Nazi-
   Soviet pact, 27; *perestroika* in,
   59; and Spanish Civil War, 19,
   20; United States and Nazi Ger-
   many as imperialists, 12; U.S.
   containment of, 100
Spanish Civil War, 19–20
Stakhanovite movement, 57
Stalin, Joseph, 20, 23–24, 32, 33
Steel industry, 52
Stock market, 58–59
Storytellers, 65
Student activism, 55, 56, 57, 110
Subacute myelo-opticoneuropathy
   (SMON), 55–56
Suffrage, 10
Sugimoto Ryōkichi, 23–24
Sugiura Jūgō, 72, 74
Sugiyama, General, 81
Sumitomo, 41, 46, 47
Suzuki Kantarō, 32, 33, 93, 96

Taishō democracy, 83, 128, 131,
   141
Tajiri Toshio, 83
Takabatake Michitoshi, 130,
   131–33
Takamatsu, Prince, 89, 98
Takeda Kiyoko, 130
Tanaka Giichi, 75, 76, 78
Tanaka Shizuichi, 83
Taniguchi, Major, 119
Tanno Setsu, 16, 17
Tax system, 49–51
Television, 60, 62–63, 65, 113,
   119, 123, 145

Tenchi, 71
Tennōssei. See Emperor system
Terasaki Hidenari, 30, 94–95, 99, 106
Tōgō Heihachirō, Admiral, 72
Tōjō Hideki, 22, 23, 29, 82–83, 88, 89, 100
Tokutomi Roka, 10, 10n
Tokyo Olympics, 53, 109, 139
Tokyo Telecommunications Engineering Corporation, 47
Tokyo war crimes trials, 28–29, 79–80, 83, 85, 94, 100, 101, 104
Tomo no kai (benevolent associations), 7–8
Tonarigumi (neighborhood associations), 42
Toranomon Incident, 9–10, 74
Tōseiha (control faction), 13, 14
Toshiba, 52
Toyoda Fukutake, 31, 32
Toyota, 51, 54, 57
Trains, 53, 59, 109
Transportation revolution, 53, 59, 65, 109
Tripartite Alliance, 22, 85–86
Tuberculosis, 37
Tukhachevsky, Marshall, 23, 24
Twenty-One-Faced Monsters case, 66, 67, 68

Uchimura Kanzō, 73
Umezu Yoshijirō, 31, 86, 87
Unions. *See* Labor unions
United Nations, 143
United States: and Allied occupation of Japan following World War II, 35–39; and arms limitations treaties, 14; automobile industry in, 51; culture of, in Japan, 6–7, 18; deaths during World War II, 30; economic sanctions against Japan, 23; Hirohito's visit to, 110, 113–14; Japanese war against, 23, 29–30, 34–35, 87–92; labor productivity in, 62; New Deal in, 12; and Persian Gulf War, 143; and Spanish Civil War, 19, 20; and Vietnam War, 53–54
U.S.-Japan Mutual Security Treaty, 52, 108, 109, 110, 130, 139, 144
Universal male suffrage act, 10
Urban culture: and automobiles, 59, 60; as consumer society, 59–60; and crime, 66–70, 139–40; housing, 60–61; and information revolution, 59–60; as information society, 64–66; in 1920s, 6–7; in 1930s, 18–19, 41; in 1960s, 40–41; and pollution, 61–62; population in urban areas, 62; and rites of passage, 63–64; and social dropouts, 62
Urban migration, 40–41, 62

Vietnam, 23
Vietnam War, 51, 53–54, 110, 130, 139

War crimes trials in Tokyo, 28–29, 79–80, 83, 85, 94, 100, 101, 104
Watanabe Masanosuke, 15
West Germany, 117, 141–42
Wolf Pack case, 66–68
Women: arrests of, under Peace

Preservation Law, 16–17; and bans on and rationing of goods, 26–27; clothing of, 26, 42, 51–52; deaths from malnutrition following World War II, 37; discrimination against, 60, 142–43; education of, 7; employment in factories, 6, 8; equal opportunity for, 60, 143; farmers' sale of daughters during Great Depression, 8; and feminist movement, 55, 142–43; GHQ reforms on, 38, 48; magazine for, 7; roles of, during World War II, 6, 27; sexuality of, 60
Workers' and Farmers' Party (Rōnōtō), 42
World War I, 73
World War II: abandoned Japanese soldiers after, 118–20; air raids against Japan, 30, 32, 33, 34–35, 44–45, 46; Allied occupation of Japan following, 35–39; atomic bombings during, 30, 33, 93, 114; bans and rationing of goods during, 25–27, 42; beginning of, in Europe, 25–26; deaths in, 29, 30; Germany's surrender, 32; Hirohito's responsibility for, 130–37, 142; Hirohito's statement calling for negotiated peace, 30–33, 44, 93–94, 125–26; impact of, 5–6; Japanese internment camps during, 113; Japanese policy toward Soviet Union during, 32–33; Japanese war against U.S., 23, 29–30, 44, 87–92, 141; Japan's

decision to ally with Hitler, 28–29; Japan's unconditional surrender, 35–39; Nazi Germany's military successes during, 27–28; Tripartite Alliance during, 22, 85–86; war crimes trials in Tokyo after, 28–29, 79–80, 83, 85, 94, 100, 101, 104; women's roles during, 6, 27. *See also* Italy; Nazi Germany; and names of specific people
Xian Incident, 21–23

Yabe Teiji, 98–99
Yalta Conference, 32
Yamamotō Gonnohyoe, 10
Yamashiro Tomoe, 16
Yanagida Kunio, 64
Yanaihara Tadao, 24
Yasuda, 41, 46
Yasukuni Shrine, 112
Yim Hyeon-Yil, 68
Yokoi Shōichi, 118–19
Yonai Mitsumasa, 32, 87, 89
Yoshida Shigeru, 87
Yoshihito, 9, 9n, 72
Yoshino Sakuzō, 73
Youth, crimes by, 66, 68–70

Zaibatsu (family-based conglomerates), 13, 38, 41, 46–47, 87
Zaitech, 58
Zenkyōtō (all-student joint struggle), 55, 56, 57
Zhang Xueliang, 21
Zhang Zuolin, 11, 13, 21, 28, 75, 76
Zhou Enlai, 21